Painting by David Sieh

SEE AND THINK AS A DESIGNER

CREATE AS A DESIGNER

SEE AND THINK AS A DESIGNER

CREATE AS A DESIGNER

CHANGING THE COLOR OF HAIR

During your career, you will have many opportunities to work with a range of clients to change and enhance their hair color. As a designer, you will be limited only by your imagination. In this course, you will discover how to design with color to create depth as well as the illusion of texture and how to draw the eye to a focal point within the hair design.

The *Color, A Designer's Approach®* program has been specially developed to help you build your skill, proficiency and confidence in color design and to prepare you for success in the salon. The foundation provided by the Pivot Point educational library you are using is built upon the individual designer's approach to learning new material and performing new skills.

A DESIGNER'S APPROACH®

COSMETOLOGY FUNDAMENTALS   **SCULPTURE**   HAIR DESIGN   COLOR   TEXTURE   SALON SUCCESS

A Designer's Approach® consists of 6 core disciplines: *Cosmetology Fundamentals, Sculpture, Hair Design, Color, Texture* and *Salon Success*, which are color-coded for easy recognition. The entire library is designed to deliver licensure-based education as well as salon-relevant training, while promoting mindful learning and future success in the salon. *A Designer's Approach* focuses on visualizing and creating color designs that are as unique as each individual client. It includes:

* Theory that gives you the thought process you'll need to guide your design decisions
* Procedures and techniques that will help you produce predictable results
* Language that allows you to think and communicate clearly with your clients and other designers

Aligning your final results with your design vision is the true benefit of using *A Designer's Approach*.

A DESIGNER'S APPROACH
REVOLVES AROUND FOUR CORNERSTONES

1 SEE   **2** THINK   **3** CREATE   **4** ADAPT

In color, to **SEE** as a designer means that you have the ability to *observe* color all around you—in fashion, nature and art as well as in hair—then *connect* these different expressions of color to one another and to the design elements and principles. Observing various expressions of color in other artistic realms and making connections will give you the inspiration to see the range of possibilities that exist for color services.

To **THINK** as a designer means that you know how to *analyze* your client's hair, features and lifestyle, *visualize* a final design, and *organize* a plan for achieving that design.

Color transformation is all about subtly or dramatically changing the color of the hair, the illusion of depth, expansion and texture within the hair. Color can play a supporting role, enhancing the overall effect of the sculpture, or it can be the focal point. You and your client will make the design decisions to create the look that will be suitable and flattering for him or her.

To **CREATE** as a designer means dedicating yourself to *practice* all aspects of color to build your expertise and to *perform* color techniques and patterns and combine them as necessary to give clients a professional salon result.

To **ADAPT** is the highest level of design proficiency. This means that you are able to *compose* innovative and artistic hair designs by drawing upon your knowledge, skill and vision. Then you can *personalize* an overall design that complements your client's individual characteristics and needs.

With *A Designer's Approach* as your "guiding principle," you have a framework for success that will last your entire career. You will see this guiding principle revealed throughout this color program.

LEARNING STRATEGIES WITHIN *COLOR*

The *Color, A Designer's Approach* coursebook has been specifically designed using state-of-the-art educational methods to make your learning process engaging as well as systematic and effective. To help you make the most of your time with your coursebook, a brief description of these learning strategies is provided here so you can become familiar with them before diving into the chapters.

First, take a look at the icons to the left. These icons will appear throughout your coursebook to help guide you through this program and help you make the most out of *Artist Access*, your online resource for all the coursebooks, video segments and other activities and learning resources.

This icon indicates that there are additional learning resources for the topic the icon is positioned with on *Artist Access*. These resources can be found by logging in to artist-access.com and navigating to the particular program and topic. These resources can range from answer keys for Brainworks activities, to supplemental workshop exercises and deeper content on some concepts presented in your coursebook.

Some exercises offer a left-handed view available exclusively on *Artist Access*. This icon invites left-handed learners to log in and navigate to the specific topic and exercise to view the technical workshop, performed by a left-handed designer.

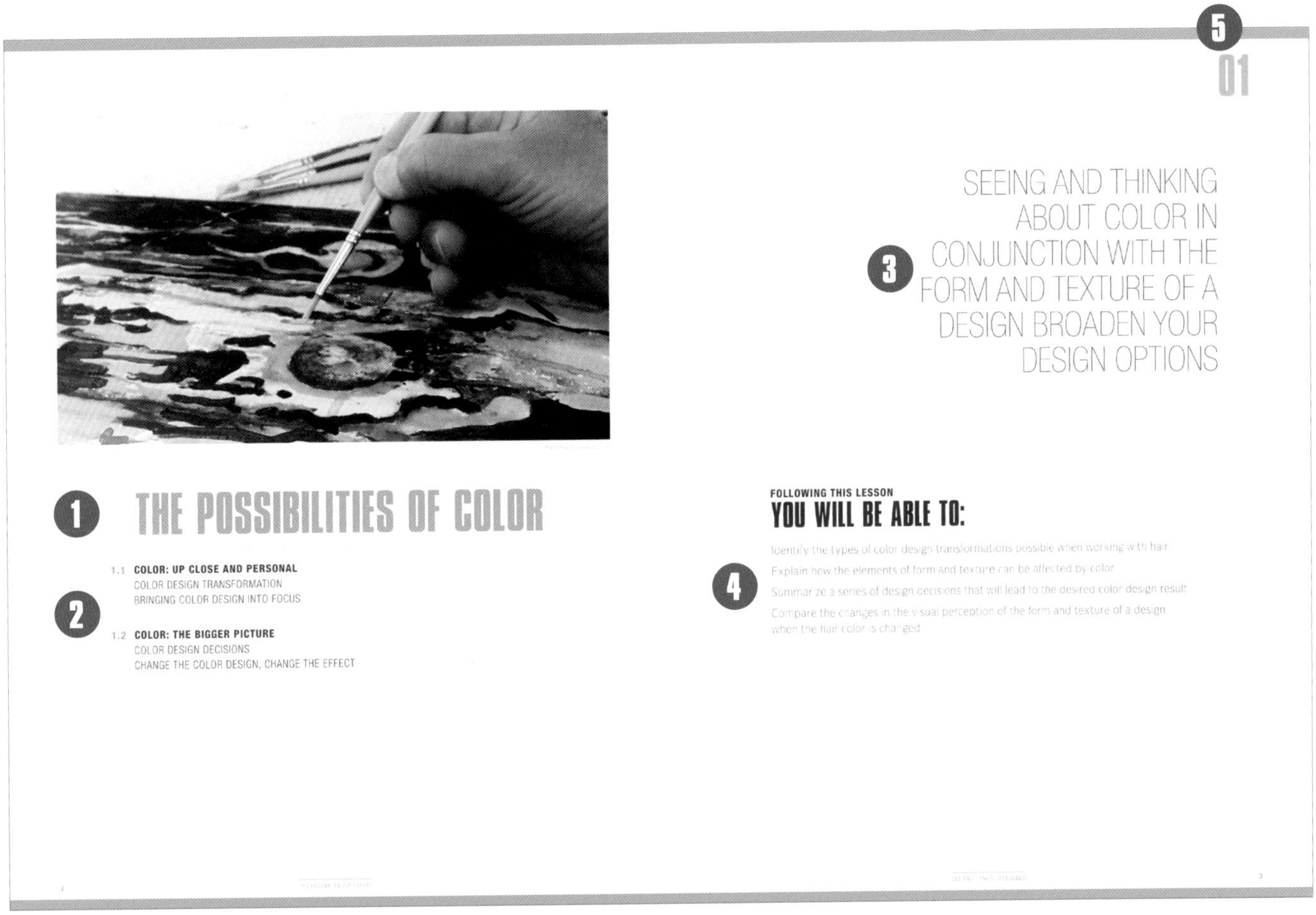
5
01
SEEING AND THINKING ABOUT COLOR IN CONJUNCTION WITH THE FORM AND TEXTURE OF A DESIGN BROADEN YOUR DESIGN OPTIONS
3
1
THE POSSIBILITIES OF COLOR
1.1 COLOR: UP CLOSE AND PERSONAL
COLOR DESIGN TRANSFORMATION
BRINGING COLOR DESIGN INTO FOCUS
2
1.2 COLOR: THE BIGGER PICTURE
COLOR DESIGN DECISIONS
CHANGE THE COLOR DESIGN, CHANGE THE EFFECT
FOLLOWING THIS LESSON
YOU WILL BE ABLE TO:
4
Identify the types of color design transformations possible when working with hair
Explain how the elements of form and texture can be affected by color
Summarize a series of design decisions that will lead to the desired color design result
Compare the changes in the visual perception of the form and texture of a design when the hair color is changed

The chapter overview is located on the first two opening pages of the chapter and provides a preview of the chapter in a concise, easy-to-read format. It contains four elements that will orient you to the chapter so you are prepared and keyed-in to the important learning concepts.

CHAPTER TITLE (1)

This is the overriding theme of the chapter.

ADVANCE ORGANIZER (2)

A "mini-outline" of the chapter headings and subheadings that identifies the main content points and provides an overall view of the chapter in its entirety.

CENTRAL MESSAGE (3)

A statement that highlights the critical value of the chapter.

LEARNING GOALS (4)

Learning outcomes that pinpoint exactly what you will learn as a result of working with the material in the chapter and preview how you will be evaluated.

SIGNATURE COLOR (5)

Each title in the *Designer's Approach* library is easily identifiable by its signature color. Shades of cyan you see on the pages as graphic treatments and titles, help identify *Color*.

Immediately following the chapter overview is an **INTROVIEW (1)**, which is an introduction to the chapter that not only previews the content, but also relates the content to you in a personal way. The introview answers questions such as, "Why is this important to me?" "Why should I care about this?" and "How will I be better off in the future as a result of understanding this subject?"

Material contained in **SIDEBARS (2)** provides examples and additional information that make the content clearer and/or more relevant to real-life salon settings.

Following each full exercise is a **DESIGN DECISIONS CHART (3)** to guide you in planning the finished design before it is executed. By filling in each of the blank sections of the chart, you will be better able to visualize the finished design composition before you even begin.

At the very end of each full exercise, **RUBRICS (4)** appear. Rubrics are self-assessment tools that help gauge your level of performance. These are designed to compare your skill and technique to industry standards.

VOICES OF SUCCESS (5) speak to you from four different and important points of view: the salon owner, the educator, the designer and the client. By capturing these industry voices, you have the advantage of discovering what is important to those people in a position to have a huge influence in your career. This creates a credible and personal bridge between your training and your career.

The primary assessment tool in each chapter is called the **LEARNING CHALLENGE (6)**. This challenge allows you to test your recall and understanding of the most important material in the chapter.

IN OTHER WORDS (7) summarizes the content with a brief statement at the end of every chapter.

LESSONS LEARNED (8) provides a list of statements that recaps the chapter's critical messages and learning objectives. These are "words of wisdom" that you can take with you throughout your career.

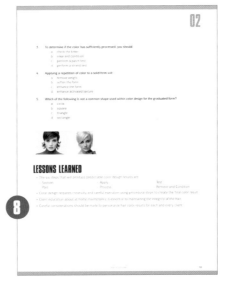

BRAINWORKS (9) are exercises that follow major learning topics and are designed to reinforce and build meaning. By working with exercises that reflect interesting or real-world situations, Brainworks allow you to relate personally to the topic and construct new meanings to affirm your understanding of the material. These exercises give you opportunities to engage in thinking about the ideas presented in the book and explore your ideas with other students.

DIVING INTO *COLOR*

Color, A Designer's Approach consists of two main areas of study: See and Think as a Designer and Create as a Designer. Each chapter within these two areas presents a discussion of key concepts, new insights on familiar topics, and practical examples. These themes build on one another from chapter to chapter. Immerse yourself in each chapter, take your time with the material, and enjoy the learning process.

SEE AND THINK AS A DESIGNER

In the first chapter, you will learn about many different aspects taken into consideration when performing color design services. These include the result you work toward as well as the specific techniques used to create those results. Your professional knowledge and personal connection with your clients will assist you in making color design decisions that will allow you to create the result you envision.

CREATE AS A DESIGNER

The second chapter of *Color, A Designer's Approach* deals with essential skills for creating successful, basic color designs using the appropriate techniques. These techniques are performed on the four basic forms.

The third chapter moves from basic to advanced color design techniques. It is in this chapter that you will use techniques adapted for combination forms as well as specialized color techniques. These techniques will help you create more inspired and personalized designs that will earn your clients' loyalty.

In the fourth chapter, the concepts of combination form color designing are used to create color designs for the male client, covering both basic and advanced techniques. You will learn to adapt the techniques you learned in Chapters 2 and 3 to suit the special needs of male clients.

ADAPT AS A DESIGNER

Pages 254-255 of this coursebook give a brief preview of what it means to adapt a color design. As skills improve, designers move beyond producing results to composing and personalizing new color designs.

Now you are ready to learn about changing the hair's color. Dive into *Color, A Designer's Approach* with enthusiasm and confidence in yourself and your teachers to prepare for a successful career.
Enjoy the journey.

EXECUTIVE MANAGEMENT

Melanie Kopeikin
President

Robert Passage
Chairman & CEO

Guy Harrington
Vice President,
Domestic Sales and Field Education

Judy Rambert
Vice President,
Education and Research

Jan Laan
Vice President,
International Business Development

Robert Sieh
Senior Vice President,
Finance and Operations

Judie Maginn
Vice President, Global Marketing
and Business Development

PRODUCTION

John Bernin
Digital Media Manager

Deidre Glover
Editorial Associate

Eileen Dubelbeis
Program Development Coordinator

Sabine Held-Perez
Senior Director, Program Development

Jen Eckstein
Marketing Manager

Melissa Holmes
Program Development Associate

Brian Fallon
Educational Content Supervisor

Amy Howard
Program Development Coordinator

Anna Fehr
Educational Technology Manager

Joanna Jakubowicz
Graphic Design Associate

Janet Fisher
Senior Director, Instructional Support

Matt McCarthy
Production Manager

Vic Piccolotto
Program Development Associate

Denise Podlin
New Products Manager

Benjamin Polk
Editorial Associate

Tina Rayyan
Production Director

Markel Richards
Program Development Associate

Rick Russell
Graphic Design Associate

Maureen Spurr
Editorial Manager

Vasiliki A. Stavrakis
Education and Research Director

Csaba Zongor
Graphic Design Associate

Robert Richards
Fashion Illustrations

Richard Weaver
Graphic Design Consultant

Painting by David Sieh

THE POSSIBILITIES OF COLOR

SEEING AND THINKING ABOUT COLOR IN CONJUNCTION WITH THE FORM AND TEXTURE OF A DESIGN BROADEN YOUR DESIGN OPTIONS

FOLLOWING THIS LESSON

YOU WILL BE ABLE TO:

———— Identify the types of color design transformations possible when working with hair

———— Explain how the elements of form and texture can be affected by color

———— Summarize a series of design decisions that will lead to the desired color design result

———— Compare the changes in the visual perception of the form and texture of a design when the hair color is changed

In today's salons, color services are such an important part of the business that many designers choose to become colorists, professionals who specialize in creating color designs.

In *Chapter 1, The Possibilities of Color*, you will learn to see and think about hair color in a way that goes far beyond shades of blond or red. You will start to understand how powerful color is as a design element. Plus, you will discover how its power provides you with unlimited creative expressions when designing color for your clients.

1.1 COLOR: UP CLOSE AND PERSONAL

Most clients, and possibly you too, think about hair color in terms of shades and simple patterns, such as:

- Blond
- Brown
- Red
- Highlights

As a true designer, you need to put hair color in context with the entire design, weighing many color options against the existing sculpted form and texture. You will then choose a color design that will best complement the overall design. Once you are able to see color as an element that works hand-in-hand with the design elements of form and texture, the ways in which you can improve your clients' appearance through color will be amazing.

# COLOR DESIGN TRANSFORMATION

There are many reasons why a client might request a color service. For example, he or she may wish to brighten the natural color, restore color that has faded from the sun, cover gray hair or make hair look fuller, just to name a few. Throughout your career as a hair designer you will see many transformations, finding a client's image dramatically altered by changing the color of the design.

Initially we will look at the range of color options as they relate to the lightness or darkness of the color as well as its shade or tonality.

You may already have noticed in the images above that color transformation is not only about changing the shade of a hair color, but also about patterns and placement of color. Based on the patterns and the color placement you choose, you can:

- Visually change or enhance the form of a design
- Visually change or enhance the texture of a design
- Create a focal point while leading the eye through a design

EFFECTS OF COLOR ON FORM

A repetition of just one color throughout a design and darker colors draws attention away from the texture of a design and focuses it on the form or silhouette.

An all-over application of a darker color draws attention to the overall form of a design.

Placing darker colors in close-fitting, narrow areas of the form and lighter colors where more expansion is desired can enhance the form of the design.

EFFECTS OF COLOR ON TEXTURE

In general, the texture of a design can either be emphasized or de-emphasized based on the color patterns and the degree of difference between the colors chosen.

One-color patterns can visually calm an otherwise activated texture.

Patterns that alternate two or more colors so that each color is clearly visible give the illusion of more texture activation.

A pattern of alternation in a selected area can help to accentuate the sculpted texture.

EFFECTS OF COLOR AS A FOCAL POINT

Selective placement of a contrasting color can create a focal point. Color can also accentuate a focal point that was created during another service, such as sculpture or hair design.

Brighter interior tones contrast with deeper tones in the perimeter, framing the face.

Subtle highlights in soft caramel tones enhance the layered texture and flatter the face with a bit of warmth.

An off-center triangle of lighter, brighter colors draws attention to the longer fringe lengths in this design.

WHEN COLOR LEADS THE EYE

artist+ access.

Take a close look at the color designs below. In your own words, state how the designs as a whole are affected by the color compositions.

BRINGING COLOR DESIGN INTO FOCUS

The perception of color is personal and subjective. What may appear as a bold hair color to one may seem rather tame to another. Learning about the fields of color enables you to communicate about color designs, leading to successful client consultations.

The five fields used to identify colors are:

- Dark
- Medium Dark
- Medium
- Medium Light
- Light

Hair colors in each field can differ in tone between:

- Neutral
- Warm
- Cool

As the images below illustrate

DARK   WARM   COOL   NEUTRAL

MEDIUM DARK

MEDIUM

MEDIUM LIGHT

WARM

COOL

NEUTRAL

LIGHT

ANALYZE THIS!

artist⁺ access.

Analyze the images below and identify which color field the hair belongs to. Then determine whether the colors shown are neutral, warm or cool in tone. Compare your assessment results with your classmates' to discover how your color perceptions differ and why it is important to use visual examples when consulting about hair color.

1.2 COLOR: THE BIGGER PICTURE

Now that you have seen all that color has to offer and you have begun to build your professional color vocabulary, it is time to look at the bigger picture so that you will be able to make appropriate design decisions. These decisions will allow you to make your vision of a color design a reality for your client.

COLOR DESIGN DECISIONS

When it comes to hair coloring, designers make decisions about hair coloring specific to the following questions:

- What are the existing and desired colors?
- How is the color supposed to affect the visual perception of the design's form?
- How is the color supposed to affect the visual perception of the design's texture?
- Which area(s) of the design should the color emphasize as a focal point?
- Which design principle works best to achieve the desired color pattern?

EXISTING/DESIRED COLOR

Clients most often come to the salon with a specific shade of color in mind. They might even go as far as communicating whether they desire highlights or an all-over color. The first step for a designer is to assess the existing hair color. Next, the designer and the client come to an agreement on the final color(s) in terms of what field it will be and which shade, whether neutral, warm or cool.

The existing dull and lackluster color is transformed to create rich, vibrant tones that are much more flattering.

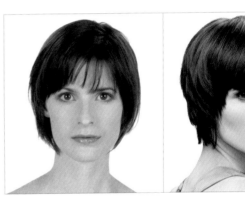

This subtle color design intensifies the overall color, and interior highlights create an illusion of surface activation.

Because everyone perceives colors differently, designers use color swatches to identify the existing hair color.

DESIGN PRINCIPLES

As you already know, design principles are artistic arrangement patterns for the design elements of:

- Form
- Texture
- Color

In color design it is critical to determine the desired design principle since this choice determines the patterns and placements to use.

REPETITION

In hair color, repetition is created by applying, or repeating, one color in a given area or throughout. This design principle is often chosen when maximum light reflection is desired.

ALTERNATION

Color alternation means that colors change from one to another repeatedly. Two or more colors can be used in an alternation to break up the light reflection and create the illusion of texture.

COLOR DESIGN DECISIONS

When it comes to hair coloring, designers make decisions about hair coloring specific to the following questions:

- What are the existing and desired colors?
- How is the color supposed to affect the visual perception of the design's form?
- How is the color supposed to affect the visual perception of the design's texture?
- Which area(s) of the design should the color emphasize as a focal point?
- Which design principle works best to achieve the desired color pattern?

EXISTING/DESIRED COLOR

Clients most often come to the salon with a specific shade of color in mind. They might even go as far as communicating whether they desire highlights or an all-over color. The first step for a designer is to assess the existing hair color. Next, the designer and the client come to an agreement on the final color(s) in terms of what field it will be and which shade, whether neutral, warm or cool.

The existing dull and lackluster color is transformed to create rich, vibrant tones that are much more flattering.

This subtle color design intensifies the overall color, and interior highlights create an illusion of surface activation.

Because everyone perceives colors differently, designers use color swatches to identify the existing hair color.

CHANGING OR ENHANCING FORM WITH COLOR

These examples illustrate how color can be used to emphasize or de-emphasize the classic characteristics of the four basic forms.

SOLID FORM

Deeper tones at the perimeter enhance the blunt form line and add visual weight.

Highlights around the face create a focal point.

Highlights throughout create the illusion of surface activation although the form remains unactivated.

GRADUATED FORM

Darker tones in the exterior enhance the tapered effect of the nape.

Interior highlights create a more activated appearance in the interior to balance the sculpted activation in the exterior.

A repetition of color throughout diminishes the contrast of the sculpted textures in the graduated form.

INCREASE-LAYERED FORM

The lighter ends showcase activated texture and the elongation of the form.

Lighter tones can be placed to create the illusion of more interior volume.

All-over highlights increase the illusion of texture activation, particularly on the long interior layers.

UNIFORMLY LAYERED FORM

A repetition of color throughout reflects the length arrangement of this sculpted form.

Highlights near the face create a focal point within the uniform lengths.

An alternation of color throughout adds to the appearance of texture activation.

CHANGING OR ENHANCING TEXTURE WITH COLOR

As stated earlier, it is the color design pattern chosen that will have the greatest effect on the perception of the overall design's texture. Note that design principles can be best used to communicate an envisioned color pattern.

The repetition of color enhances the unactivated texture of this solid form.

An alternation of colors on the surface creates the illusion of texture activation.

The use of a single color helps this layered form look calmer and less activated.

The alternation of colors in this design exaggerates the texture activation in the interior.

Interior and exterior colors contrast to reflect the contrasting textures in this graduated design.

Interior highlights add the illusion of texture activation to visually reduce the amount of texture contrast.

DESIGN PRINCIPLES

As you already know, design principles are artistic arrangement patterns for the design elements of:

- Form
- Texture
- Color

In color design it is critical to determine the desired design principle since this choice determines the patterns and placements to use.

REPETITION

In hair color, repetition is created by applying, or repeating, one color in a given area or throughout. This design principle is often chosen when maximum light reflection is desired.

ALTERNATION

Color alternation means that colors change from one to another repeatedly. Two or more colors can be used in an alternation to break up the light reflection and create the illusion of texture.

PROGRESSION

Progression in hair color refers to an ascending or descending scale of colors. These colors can progress from lighter to darker and/or from warmer to cooler.

CONTRAST

Contrast describes a relationship of opposites, which creates interest, variety and excitement in a color design. Contrasting colors need to be at least three levels apart from one another. Darker colors create depth, while lighter colors seem to come forward, sometimes creating the illusion of volume.

COLOR PLACEMENT

It is essential to place color in a way to best complement the shape and expansion of the design as well as the desired movement and texture in the finished look. Many salons operate with a separate color department where colorists solely perform these services. In these settings, it is critical that the communication between the colorist and the stylist is efficient and utilizes commonly shared and consistent terminology.

When colorists communicate about the color designs with peers or customers, they usually describe color placement in terms of zones and shapes as well as placement of color along the strand.

COLOR WITHIN ZONES

Zones are segmented areas of a design that are colored separately. One color can be applied throughout the zone, or the zones can be separated into shapes.

The simplest form of a zonal pattern is created when one color is applied throughout the entire head as one zone.

Often, the head is divided into two zones with a different color or technique applied throughout each one. This pattern is effective when a focal point or area is desired.

Several zones can be colored with shades that gradually become lighter or darker. This zonal pattern is effective for leading the eye through a design toward a specific area, or to create a natural-looking progression of color.

COLOR WITHIN SHAPES

When desired patterns are more intricate and require that smaller strands of hair be colored differently, shapes are used to further break down the zones. Geometric shapes are used to effectively describe sectioning and parting patterns used in color designs. These shapes are then further subdivided by partings. Within each shape one or multiple colors can be applied. Shapes commonly used in color designs are:

- Rectangles
- Triangles
- Circles

RECTANGLE

A rectangle is often positioned at the top of the head to create an alternation of colors.

TRIANGLE

Triangles can be positioned anywhere on the head and, depending on the technique chosen, any design principle can be achieved.

CIRCLE

A circle is a closed, curved shape that is often positioned at the top of the head or crown. Alternating or repeating patterns can be used with pivotal partings throughout the circle.

COLOR ALONG THE STRAND

In addition to using zones and shapes, the placement of the color along the strand, in relation to the length of the hair and the sculpted form, can create specific patterns. Color can be applied anywhere along the strand depending on the desired effect.

The most common applications are:
- Base to ends
- Base
- Away from the base
- Ends
- Combinations of any of these

BASE TO ENDS

Generally, designers use a base-to-ends color application to create a new color along the entire strand.

BASE

With the base technique, color can be applied to the new growth to match an existing color. Designers, however, often use the base technique to intentionally apply a different color in order to create a specific effect.

AWAY FROM THE BASE

Color can be applied away from the base to create a somewhat grown-out effect and to avoid a hard line as the color grows out. This is particularly desirable when clients are worried about high-maintenance upkeep of a color. Applying away from the base is also the first part of the virgin-lighter application technique.

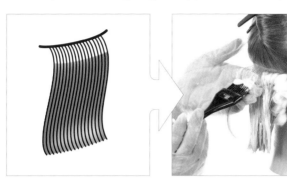 

ENDS

To accentuate the activated texture of a design, color can be applied to the ends.

COMBINATION

When dimensional and textural effects are desired, a combination of application techniques can be used. For example, darker color can be used at the base to create depth, while lighter ends can showcase activated texture.

CHANGE THE COLOR DESIGN, CHANGE THE EFFECT

By now you have developed an awareness of the positive effects a color design can have on a client's appearance, affecting how she or he looks and feels.

Color design can be the "icing on the cake" for a hair sculpture, adding drama while accentuating the cut. The alternation of colors in the interior of the design is somewhat bold, but does not overpower the uniqueness of the sculpture.

Sometimes a client will want a truly dramatic color transformation—creating a whole new image. It can be exciting to be part of such a daring change. Careful planning and skillful application can create stunning results!

Not every color design is intended to be noticed or recognized. Subtly reducing the amount of gray can help a client look and feel younger without being obvious and without tell-tale "roots" that give away the secret. This kind of subtle, "unnoticeable" color design can win you some of the most steady and loyal clients!

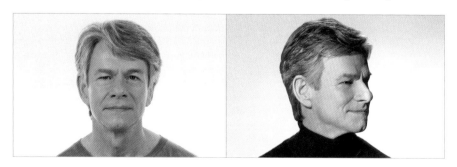

COLOR DECISIONS

Combine the color concepts you have just learned with your artistic abilities and color the design below. Before you reach for your colored pencils, crayons and/or markers, identify the sculpted form and the existing texture. Then decide in what way your color design should impact both. After coloring, identify the design principle you chose for your color pattern.

FORM: _____

TEXTURE: _____

DESIGN PRINCIPLE: _____

VOICES OF SUCCESS

"It can be very hard to offer clients something new on a regular basis, especially when they aren't open to cutting their hair shorter. Thankfully, color allows me to transform my client's look over and over, from subtle to dramatic. My clients know I always have a new idea to offer, and I can keep them excited about their next visit."

THE DESIGNER

"Color makes up a large percentage of our salon's income. I insist on a thorough understanding about color design options. We make sure the color designs we offer go beyond what a client could do at home or what any salon down the street can offer."

THE SALON OWNER

"Sometimes students don't really know where to start with a color consultation and what questions to ask. Knowing the color design decisions really helps them when having that conversation with their client. Knowing professional color design terminology also allows them to express their creative ideas with confidence."

THE EDUCATOR

IN OTHER WORDS

Color offers an abundance of creative options. By knowing how color affects form and texture, you can create color designs that have a positive impact on your clients' appearance and the way they feel.

LEARNING CHALLENGE

Circle the letter corresponding to the correct answer.

1. Based on the color patterns and placement chosen, designers can visually change the hair design's:
    a. length
    b. overall volume
    c. texture and form
    d. finishing direction

2. A repetition of just one color throughout a design and darker colors draw attention away from the texture of a design and focus it on the:
    a. design line
    b. form or silhouette
    c. movement of the design
    d. focal point in the design

3. The texture of a design can either be emphasized or de-emphasized based on the choice of color patterns and:
    a. field
    b. tonality
    c. processing time
    d. the degree of difference between the colors

4. The first step during the color design decision process is to assess:
    a. the existing hair color
    b. the desired color pattern
    c. the desired color placement
    d. the design principle to be used

5. Applying one color within a given area or throughout results in:
    a. contrast
    b. repetition
    c. alternation
    d. progression

LESSONS LEARNED

- Color design allows the designer to visually transform the perception of a design's form and texture.

- Color needs to be used in context with the entire design, weighing the abundance of color options against the elements of form and texture.

- Making color design decisions and communicating them using professional terminology will increase clients' confidence in you as their designer and in the finished color result.

- Design principles serve as arrangement patterns in color design based on which color patterns and placements are chosen.

- Intentionally placing color along selective strands of the hair increases creative color options.

BASIC COLOR DESIGN

CREATING PREDICTABLE COLOR DESIGN RESULTS REQUIRES A STEP-BY-STEP PROCESS

FOLLOWING THIS LESSON

YOU WILL BE ABLE TO:

Describe the six procedural steps used to achieve predictable color design results

Explain the importance of guidelines for maintaining the integrity of the hair when coloring

Explain the importance of guidelines for ensuring client comfort and satisfaction when performing a color design service

Explain various color design options for the four basic forms

Demonstrate the knowledge and ability to perform various color designs on the four basic forms

Trained designers help guide their hair color clients by listening to their concerns and offering suggestions. They also narrow the available color selections by discussing color placement and patterns that can be used. It takes careful consideration, a trained eye, and a well-planned set of procedural steps to create desirable color results time after time.

In *Chapter 2, Basic Color Design*, you will learn the procedural steps used to perform many sought-after color designs on the four basic forms. You will learn color placement and special considerations to accommodate your clients while learning how to teach them to maintain their color at home.

2.1 ESSENTIAL COLOR DESIGN TECHNIQUES

When you learn how to design and perform color design services, you will need to develop your ability to visualize color placement and color patterns. You will also need to take into consideration the structure of the hair sculpture you are creating your color design upon. You will learn to master this combination of creative and technical skills and how to apply this knowledge by performing essential color design techniques.

PREDICTABLE COLOR DESIGN RESULTS

Consulting with your clients about the color choices they have in mind is just the start to designing color. To create successful color designs, you'll need to consider the existing color of the hair as well as the density, porosity and growth patterns. After completing this assessment, you will then choose specific techniques to achieve predictable color results.

COLOR DESIGN SERVICES

DESIGNERS FOLLOW THESE SIX COLOR STEPS AS THE FOUNDATION OF THEIR COLOR DESIGNS:

① SECTION

② PART

③ APPLY

④ PROCESS

⑤ TEST

⑥ REMOVE AND CONDITION

① SECTION

Sectioning is used to help map out the placement of color and positioning of foils, and can isolate the area of the design that is going to be accentuated. To achieve the most desirable effects, a thorough analysis of the hair sculpture is needed to see where the lengths will fall when the hair is styled so the color will be placed in the most desirable areas. Designers use geometric shapes to identify sections in hair coloring.

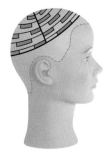

RECTANGULAR shapes can be used to create a distinct alternation of colors. They are often positioned to correlate to a center or side part and may extend through the crown.

CIRCULAR shapes can be used within a design to help distinguish color patterns between the exterior and interior of a hair design.

TRIANGULAR shapes can be used to isolate sections of hair in the fringe to add interest in a specific focal area.

② PART

In color design, parting allows you to determine how evident the color pattern is in the final result. The direction and thickness of the parting can determine how bold or subtle the color will appear. For example, horizontal slices placed in the interior will create a definite alternation of color while diagonal slices will create a more blended effect. Partings can be taken with straight lines resulting in slices, or the partings can be woven, as is commonly done for highlights. The thickness of the parting is determined by considering the product to be used, the hair density—to ensure proper penetration of color—and the desired boldness or subtleness of the color pattern.

PARTING DIRECTIONS

Any lines from the celestial axis can be used to identify parting directions, which include:

- Horizontal
- Vertical
- Diagonal
- Pivotal
- Concave
- Convex

HORIZONTAL

VERTICAL

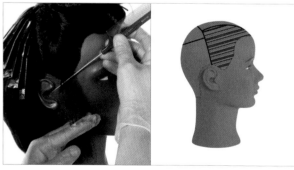

DIAGONAL

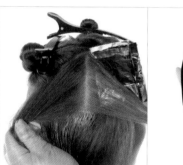 

PIVOTAL

Zigzag partings can also be used to allow a greater transition between zones. The steeper the zigzag parting, the more blended the final result will appear.

WEAVING

Dimensional hair coloring is most commonly achieved by introducing one or more colors selectively within a design. Strands to be highlighted or lowlighted are usually selected by parting a straight line, then weaving off the top of the parting. The woven strands are generally enclosed in foil or thermal strips to isolate them from the remaining hair.

COLOR RECORDING SYSTEM

DENSITY PATTERN	SIZE OF WEAVE		
	FINE	MEDIUM	THICK
LIGHT			
MEDIUM			
HEAVY			

The size of the weave refers to the amount of hair selected, while the density of the pattern refers to the number of weaves within a particular area. Keep in mind that the depth of a weave also influences the amount of hair selected.

FINE   MEDIUM   THICK (CHUNKY)

SLICING

Slicing is also considered a dimensional hair coloring technique. Similar to weaving, in this technique strands to be highlighted or lowlighted are selected by parting a straight line, or slicing through the hair. Generally, these strands are then enclosed in foil or thermal strips to isolate them from the remaining hair.

COLOR RECORDING SYSTEM

DENSITY PATTERN	SIZE OF SLICE		
	FINE	MEDIUM	THICK
LIGHT			
MEDIUM			
HEAVY			

The size of a slice refers to the amount of hair selected, while the density of the pattern refers to the number of slices within a particular area.

As a general rule, the finer the slice, the more blended the appearance. The thicker the slice, the bolder the color appearance.

Slices can also be positioned one on top of another, referred to as a back-to-back technique.

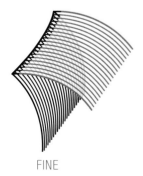

FINE

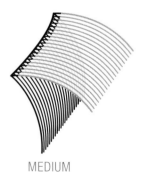

MEDIUM

THICK

③ APPLY

Since most clients will sit in front of a mirror while color is applied, it is important to make sure the application is neat and organized to make the client feel more comfortable and to prevent staining of the scalp and skin. As clients watch the application and see it happening with ease and accuracy, their trust grows along with their excitement for successful results.

APPLICATION TOOLS

Other considerations include deciding which tool or tools you will use to apply the color.

Using a color bowl and brush is a popular way to apply permanent colors and lighteners, while demi-permanent colors and toners are more likely to be applied with an applicator bottle. As you gain more experience, you may find that you favor one application tool over another.

When weaving or slicing, different products such as cream-based conditioners or barrier creams are sometimes applied to isolate the hair that will not be treated with color. Aluminum foils and thermal strips are commonly used to help enclose the colored weaves or slices.

When positioning foils, ensure that the foil is close to the scalp and secured. If the foil slips, or product travels beyond the edge of the foil, color seepage will occur. This causes a colored line near the base, often referred to as "bleeding."

COLOR ALONG THE STRAND

As discussed in *Chapter 1, The Possibilities of Color*, knowing where to apply the color along the strand plays a big role in achieving the desired results.

COMMON AREAS TO APPLY COLOR ALONG THE STRAND ARE:

BASE TO ENDS

When applying color from base to ends, it is important to ensure that the product thoroughly penetrates the entire strand. Areas of the strand that absorb less color will look uneven and have a "spotted" result.

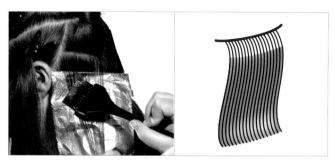

AWAY FROM BASE

Color can be applied away from the base to create a grown-out or "lived-in" effect. This technique is popular with clients who desire a natural-looking result with less required upkeep. Note that holding the brush at an angle while applying color away from the base results in an even softer color transition.

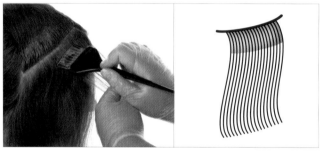

BASE

Applying color to the base of the hair is generally referred to as a retouch application. The selected color should match the existing color on the hair.

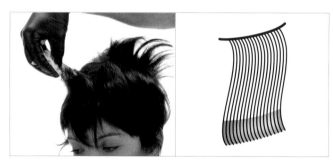

ENDS

Often this technique is performed on shorter hair using lightener to achieve a "sun-kissed" look. Applying a different color to the ends of the hair within an activated texture will visually enhance the appearance of the activation.

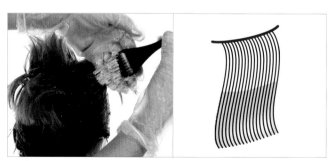

COMBINATION

Clients who love to wear expressive hair colors will often want a design in which a combination of techniques needs to be used.

NEATNESS IS KEY!
It's important to remember not to overlap the color onto previously colored hair. When coloring hair darker, overlapping beyond the new growth results in a darker "band." When lightener is applied beyond the new growth onto previously lightened hair, breakage could result.

In addition, the designer needs to choose where to start the color application based on the needed processing time and desired final result. When creating a darker result, designers often begin the color application in the area that naturally would be the darkest. If a lighter result is desired, designers often begin the application in the area that naturally would be the lightest. In other instances, designers may choose to begin applying in the area where the greatest color change is needed to allow for longer processing.

 PROCESS

Once the color has been applied it is time for the products to process. At this point you will immediately remove any excess color along the hairline, ears and neck to avoid creating a dark line or shadow.

The color products should be timed according to manufacturer's instructions, while considering the hair's porosity. In general, porous hair has the ability to absorb more product more quickly. During a color service, this means that porous hair often processes faster and has a tendency to turn out darker.

For example, while performing a toner application after highlights, it is important to carefully monitor the color development on the hair, since prelightening has made the hair more porous and more absorbent. On the other hand, when working with resistant hair that has less-than-average porosity, such as gray hair, you may decide to apply heat for a more even color result.

⑤ TEST

A strand test will help determine whether the color products have sufficiently processed and allow you to see if the color has developed successfully. Multiple areas may need to be tested multiple times during processing. For example, when highlighting, you may need to look at the first foils placed before you have finished placing the last few foils. Depending on the time it takes to apply all the foils, the first few may already have processed sufficiently and need to be removed.

⑥ REMOVE AND CONDITION

Once you have achieved the desired color and processing is complete, you will remove the color products thoroughly from the hair and scalp, in most cases by rinsing and shampooing prior to conditioning the hair. You will also discuss with your client different home care products he or she can use to maintain salon-style results between appointments.

WHAT'S GOING ON?

Analyze the images below and determine which procedural step is shown.

PRACTICE
MAKES PERFECT 01
VIRGIN-DARKER
TECHNIQUE

The focus of this exercise is to provide practice in the techniques most often used to apply a repetition of color to add tone and/or darken a given area or an entire design. A base-to-ends color application is used to deposit color on natural hair for the first time or to darken previously colored hair.

Practice this exercise to build rhythm, skill, speed and consistency in the virgin-darker technique using ¼" (.6 cm) diagonal-back partings applying product from base to ends.

Use previously colored hair swatches to predict the results you will achieve.

Here, a medium red-orange is chosen to darken and add warmth to this light field.

FORMULA: *Level 6, red-orange demi-permanent color with developer.*

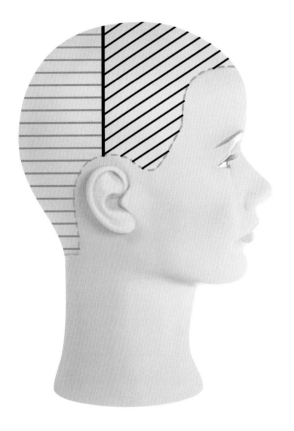

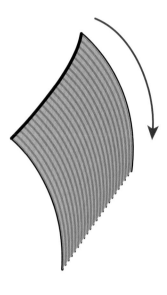

The traditional sectioning pattern divides the head into four basic sections from the center front hairline to the nape and from ear to ear. Each section is subdivided into ¼" (.6 cm) horizontal or diagonal partings.

The color product will be applied from base to ends.

01 Begin by applying barrier cream around the hairline and top of the ear to prevent staining.

02–03 Apply barrier cream to the surrounding quadrants, then apply foil over the barrier cream.

04 Begin the color application at the top. Take a ¼" (.6 cm) diagonal-back parting.

05 Apply color from base to ends. Apply to the top and bottom of each parting to ensure even coverage. Direct strands up and away from the face.

06–07 Work toward the bottom of the section. Apply from the base to the ends of each parting.

08 As the partings become wider, subdivide them for control. Work neatly and apply product evenly from base to ends.

09 Continue to apply product to the top and bottom of each parting using the base-to-ends technique.

10 Continue working downward while subdividing for control.

11 Direct the last strand away from the face and apply color carefully to protect the face from color staining.

12 Carefully outline the hairline to ensure even coverage.

13 A wide-tooth comb may be used to evenly distribute the color through the hair. Allow the color to develop.

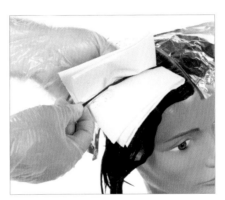

14–15 To strand test for color development, lay a small section of hair along a white paper towel and spray the hair with water. Rub gently across the strand to remove product from base to ends. Then, use a clean towel to check the ends against the base for even color development. Once the desired color has been achieved, rinse, shampoo, condition and finish as desired.

16 Consistent application will ensure even coverage from base to ends.

17 The finished color displays rich, medium warm tones that are even from base to ends.

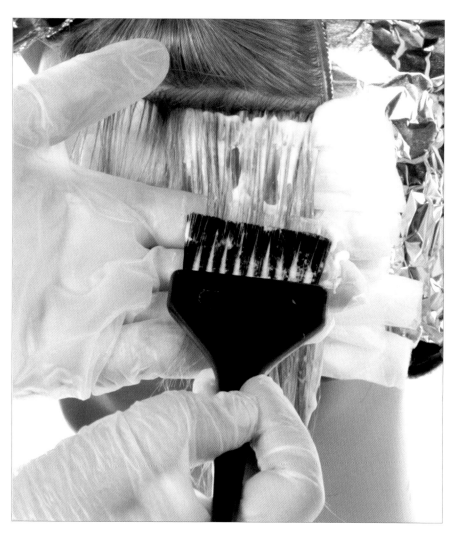

PRACTICE
MAKES PERFECT 02
VIRGIN-LIGHTER
TECHNIQUE

The focus of this exercise is to provide practice in the techniques most often used to apply lightener to hair for the first time. A double-process application allows the colorist to create a new pigment foundation upon which to build lighter colors not always obtainable with a single process.

Practice this exercise to build rhythm, skill, speed and consistency in the virgin-lighter technique using ⅛" (.3 cm) and ¼" (.6 cm) diagonal-back partings.

When lightening hair for the first time, heat from the scalp will speed up the lifting action at the base. Processing time is adjusted by applying product ½" (1.25 cm) away from the scalp first. When the hair is halfway to the desired degree of lightness, newly mixed product is then applied to the base. Determining the final color result first allows you to assess the amount of decolorizing necessary. This medium field was decolorized to pale yellow and then recolorized with a light violet to create a light, neutral blond.

FORMULA: *On-the-scalp cream lightener; 10 volume (3%) developer.* TONER: *Level 10, violet-based permanent color with 10 volume (3%) developer.*

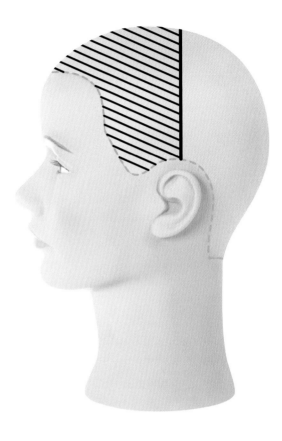

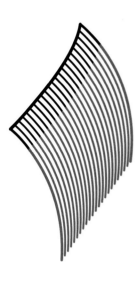

The art shows ⅛" (.3 cm) diagonal-back partings used throughout this exercise. Lightener will be applied ½" (1.25 cm) away from the scalp through the midstrand, and up to or through the ends, depending on the condition of the hair. Product will then be applied to the base. If the ends are very porous, you may choose to apply product to this part of the strand last.

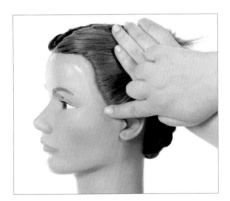

01 Begin by applying barrier cream around the hairline and top of the ear.

02–03 Outline the remaining quadrants with barrier cream, and cover with foil to protect the hair that will not be treated.

04–05 Begin at the bottom of the section. Take a ⅛" (.3 cm) diagonal-back parting. Apply lightener ½" (1.25 cm) away from the scalp, through the midstrand and ends, completely saturating the hair. Place cotton at the base to prevent product seepage. Work neatly and apply product evenly.

06 Work upward. Subdivide partings for control as they become wider.

07 Note that you may apply lightener to the top and bottom of each strand depending on hair density and the consistency of the product to achieve even saturation.

08 Continue to the top of the section, making sure the lightener is applied consistently.

09 Strand test frequently for the desired degree of decolorization. Use water and a damp towel to remove the lightener. Compare color against a white towel.

10–11 When the hair is halfway to the desired level, remove the cotton and apply fresh product to the base of each strand. Work from the top to the bottom and subdivide the partings for control if necessary. Work neatly, applying product to one or both sides of the strand.

12 Reapply around the hairline to ensure even and thorough coverage.

13 Bring each section down to allow for proper oxidation and to cross-check your application. Then process until you reach the desired level of decolorization.

14 Rinse, shampoo with light manipulations, condition and dry the hair.

15 The hair shows even decolorization from base to ends. If the hair color is not even, reapply lightener where necessary.

16–17 Reapply barrier cream and foil around the section. Begin at the top using ¼" (.6 cm) diagonal-back partings. Apply the color, also known as a toner, from base to ends. Apply color to both sides of each strand as needed to ensure complete coverage. Work for a clean application, subdividing as necessary.

18 Reapply around the hairline to ensure even coverage.

19 Bring the hair down to allow for oxidation and to check your application. Allow the color to develop, and strand test to verify results.

20 Rinse, shampoo, condition and finish as desired. The results show even color from base to ends.

21 The result will reflect the color chosen. This result produced a light, neutral blond by using a light violet-based toner.

PRACTICE MAKES PERFECT 03
WEAVING – HIGHLIGHT TECHNIQUE

The focus of this exercise is to provide practice in a common technique used to create highlights in the hair. Highlights create an alternation of a lighter color on a darker base color, breaking up the light reflection and increasing the appearance of surface texture. In this exercise, selected strands are woven and isolated in foil while product is applied and processed.

Practice this exercise to build rhythm, skill, speed and consistency in the weaving-highlight technique using ½" (1.25 cm) horizontal partings.

Determining the desired color result for the highlights first allows you to assess the necessary amount of decolorization.

In this exercise, a medium-fine weave was used to highlight this dark field, lifting the woven strands to a medium light color.

FORMULA: *On-the-scalp cream lightener; 20 volume (6%) developer.* TONER: *Level 10, violet-based permanent color with 10 volume (3%) developer.*

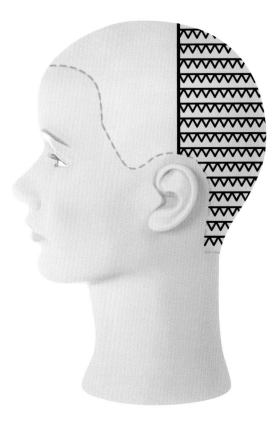

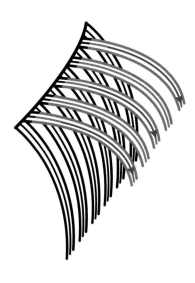

There are many sectioning and parting patterns used for highlighting. In this exercise, ½" (1.25 cm) horizontal partings are used with a medium-fine weave.

01 Take a ½" (1.25 cm) horizontal parting in the nape. Then part a thin section off the top and use a tail comb to create a medium-fine weave.

02–03 While holding the selected strands, fold the end of the foil over the tail of the comb. Position the foil under the woven strands with the fold positioned toward the scalp.

04–05 Hold the hair taut and apply color away from the edge of the foil at first to avoid seepage, then apply to the edge of the foil. Position your palm under the foil as you continue to apply product through the ends.

06 Then fold the foil upward to the parting.

07 Lift the foil and reinforce its position close to the scalp with the tail of the comb. This will help to prevent product seepage.

08–09 Use the comb to fold each side toward the center, keeping the foil packet the same width as the woven strands. The foil keeps the lightener isolated from the hair that is to remain untreated. The tail of the comb may also be used to fold the foil.

10–11 Work upward. Take a thin section from the top of each ½" (1.25 cm) horizontal parting, then create a medium-fine weave. Remember to apply the product away from the foil edge first, then to the edge of the foil.

12 When the sections become too wide, subdivide for control using a bricklay pattern.

13–14 Continue to work upward taking ½" (1.25 cm) horizontal partings. Then part and weave a thin section from the top of each parting.

15–16 Be sure to position each foil close to the scalp and reinforce the position after product is applied, especially working over the curves of the head, to help prevent product seepage.

17 The completed application shows an alternation of foils and hair that will remain untreated.

18 Process until the desired degree of lightness is achieved. Then remove the foils, rinse, shampoo and condition. Finish the hair as desired.

19 The finish shows an alternation of the pre-existing color and the lightened strands throughout.

PRACTICE
MAKES PERFECT 04
SLICING –
LOWLIGHT
TECHNIQUE

The focus of this exercise is to provide practice in the techniques most often used to apply a darker color to selected strands using the slicing technique. This technique is referred to as lowlighting and is used to create depth within a design. Lowlights are very often combined with highlights.

Practice this exercise to build rhythm, skill, speed and consistency in the slicing technique using ¼" (.6 cm) diagonal-back partings, applying product away from the base to the ends.

Using your previously colored quadrant, choose a color that will add darker tones. In this exercise, you will learn another technique for lowlighting or highlighting called slicing. This technique incorporates straight partings.

FORMULA: *Level 5, red-violet demi-permanent color with developer.*

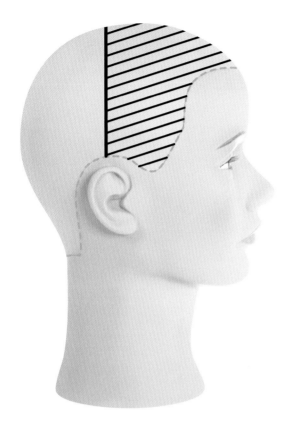

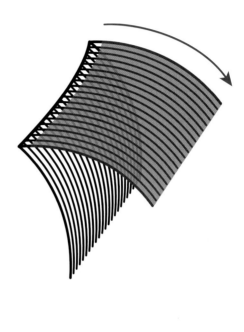

There are many parting patterns that can be used, depending on the desired results. Here, a diagonal-back parting pattern with thin partings, or slices, is used.

In this exercise, product is applied away from the scalp to the ends.

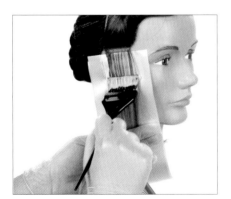

01–02 Begin at the front hairline with a diagonal-back parting at the bottom of the section. This hair will be left natural. Apply barrier cream to the base area then cover with a thermal strip. Note that the hair that will remain the existing color is double the thickness of the lowlights.

03 Next, take a fine slice and clip the remaining hair up out of the way. Begin applying the darker color near the edge of the thermal strip.

04–05 Continue applying color through to the ends. Cover with another thermal strip. Release another parting. Apply barrier cream to the hair left natural. Continue to alternate between natural and lowlighted hair. Note that the thermal strips are not folded.

06–07 As the partings become wider, subdivide using two thermal strips as you continue to alternate the natural hair with the lowlights. Apply the color away from the edge of the thermal strip to the ends. Then cover with thermal strips.

08 Work to the top of the section. Note that the last parting will be left natural.

09 Allow the color to develop. Rinse, shampoo, condition and finish as desired.

10 The finish shows an alternation of darker red lowlights adding depth and increasing the illusion of activation.

PRACTICE MAKES PERFECT 05
GRAY REDUCTION WEAVING TECHNIQUE

The focus of this exercise is to provide practice in the techniques most often used to reduce the appearance of gray using a weaving technique. In a gray reduction service, selected strands are lowlighted, or colored darker, using the weaving or slicing technique. A color close to the client's pigmented hair is usually chosen for a more natural appearance.

Practice this exercise to build rhythm, skill, speed and consistency in the weaving technique using horizontal partings and applying product away from the scalp to the ends.

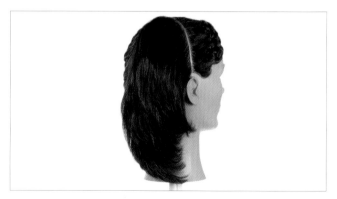

To ensure predictable results, use colored swatches to determine the color and tone to be used. Here a medium dark, warm brown was used on a dark gray field. A medium-weave technique was used throughout.

FORMULA: *Level 6, gold with level 4, natural permanent color with 20 volume (6%) developer.*

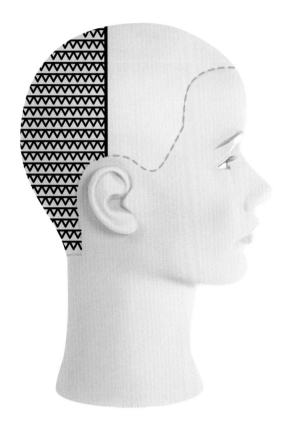

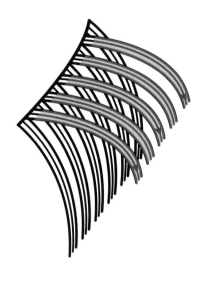

While many patterns can be used, generally horizontal partings are used in the back, and diagonal-back partings can be used at the sides.

The color product will be applied away from the scalp to the ends using a medium-weaving technique.

01 Begin at the nape using horizontal partings and clipping the remaining hair for control. Distribute each parting, then use the tail of the comb to create a medium weave off the top of the parting.

02–03 Position the foil at the scalp under the woven strands. Apply the color away from the edge of the foil first, then from the edge of the foil to the ends.

04–05 Use the double-fold technique, folding approximately ⅓ upward, then folding up to the parting. Use the tail of your comb to reinforce the position of the foil close to the scalp to prevent product seepage.

06 Use the teeth of the tail comb to crease and fold each side inward.

07–08 Work upward using horizontal partings and the medium-weave technique. When partings become too wide, subdivide for control. Apply product away from the scalp to the ends. Fold the foil upward twice and reinforce the position of the foil. Then use the comb to crease and fold the sides inward.

09 Work to the top of the section.

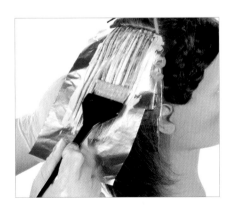

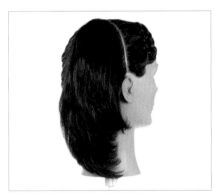

10 Apply from the edge of each foil to the ends and use the double-fold technique.

11 Allow the color to develop. Remove the foils, rinse, shampoo, condition and finish as desired.

12 The finish shows an effective, natural-looking amount of gray reduction.

PRACTICE MAKES PERFECT 06
GRAY COVERAGE RETOUCH TECHNIQUE

The focus of this exercise is to provide practice in the techniques most often used to apply color to the new growth of hair that has been previously colored. A retouch application is usually performed when approximately ½" (1.25 cm) of new growth is evident or approximately every 4-6 weeks. A color matching the pre-existing color is required.

Practice this exercise to build rhythm, skill, speed and consistency in the retouch technique, using horizontal partings while applying product to the new growth only.

Complete gray coverage is a result of appropriate color formulation. Your previously colored swatches may be considered a preliminary strand test for the selection of color you will use in this exercise. Here a dark warm brown was used on the quadrant previously used in the gray reduction exercise.

FORMULA: *Level 6, gold with level 4, natural permanent color with 20 volume (6%) developer.*

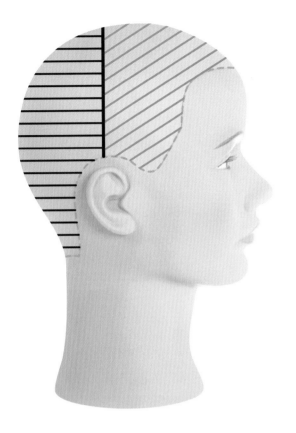

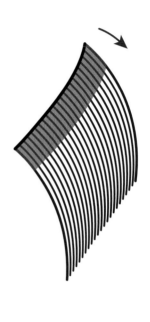

While many patterns can be used to perform a retouch application, generally horizontal partings are used in the back, while diagonal-back partings are used at the sides.

The color product will be applied to the ½" (1.25 cm) of new growth.

01 Isolate the unused quadrants and protect the hair with barrier cream and foil. Apply barrier cream around the hairline to protect the skin and prevent staining.

02–03 To create a simulation of a client needing a retouch, begin at the nape using ¼" (.6 cm) partings. Apply color ½" (1.25 cm) away from the scalp through to the ends. Position cotton between the partings to prevent the color from staining the uncolored hair.

04–05 As you work upward, subdivide the partings for control and continue to use the same technique. Allow the color to develop. Then rinse, shampoo, condition and dry the hair.

06 Refer to the client's record card. Assess if any changes in formulation are needed. If no changes are necessary, duplicate the formula previously used.

07–08 To prepare for the retouch application, protect the untreated quadrants with barrier cream and foil. Apply barrier cream around the hairline. Begin at the top and take a ¼" (.6 cm) horizontal parting. Apply color to the new growth only. If necessary, apply product to the top and bottom of the parting.

09 Use the same technique on subsequent partings. Apply product only to the area of the hair that is uncolored. Avoid overlapping product onto previously colored hair.

Overlapping product onto the previously colored hair will cause a darker line from additional deposit.

 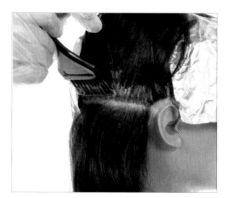

10 Based on the client's hair density, you may choose to apply color to the top or to the top and bottom of each parting.

11 Work toward the nape and subdivide partings for control as needed.

12 Continue to take ¼" (.6 cm) partings and apply product to the new growth only.

13 To ensure even coverage, outline the hairline.

14 Beginning at the nape, bring each section down to allow the color to oxidize.

15 Allow the color to develop. Rinse, shampoo, condition and finish as desired.

16 The result displays even coverage from base to ends. Rich tones and beautiful, natural color can be achieved for clients with gray hair.

If your client's color has faded along the midstrand or lost its vibrancy, it will be necessary to refresh the color during a retouch service. This can be accomplished by distributing the remaining color throughout the entire strand for the last 5-10 minutes of processing time. Or, you may wish to formulate and apply a deposit-only color gloss in a matching shade throughout the midstrand and ends. Color-enhancing shampoo and/or conditioner can be recommended to help maintain color between salon visits.

GUIDELINES FOR CLIENT-CENTERED COLOR DESIGN

Client-centered guidelines are designed to help you do everything possible to enhance your client's comfort and satisfaction. Combining your experience with predictable color design results and client-centered guidelines will ensure exceptional color results and a pleasant experience for your clients.

PROCEDURAL GUIDELINES

The following chart will help you ensure your client's comfort and safety during the color service.

 SECTION
- Explain to client that you are using a sectioning pattern that is specifically designed to achieve desired results
- Consider sculpture, texture and position of weight and volume in the hair design
- Consider natural growth patterns and density, and adjust sections if needed

 PART
- Explain to client how the direction and width of the parting will affect the color results

 APPLY
- Work neatly and accurately. so the client doesn't have to worry about stains on the skin, color "bleeding" or overlapping colors

 PROCESS
- Maintain client comfort by ensuring cape is on the outside back of the chair and draping is secure
- Inform client of the approximate processing time
- Remove color from skin around the hairline to prevent staining
- Offer beverage or reading material to client while processing
- Check on your clients during processing so they won't feel forgotten

 TEST
- Explain to the client that you are ensuring the color has developed successfully prior to rinsing
- Perform a strand test in various areas of the design, especially when working on hair with different degrees of porosity

 REMOVE AND CONDITION
- Ensure the client's neck is comfortably positioned in the shampoo bowl while rinsing
- Avoid strong manipulations since the scalp may be sensitive, and ask client if water temperature is comfortable
- Position your hand to shield the client's face and ears while rinsing
- Inform clients of the importance of at home care

COMMUNICATION GUIDELINES

The following chart will help you respond to the most common client cues in a way that encourages client trust, loyalty and open communication.

CLIENT CUE	DESIGNER RESPONSE
"My scalp has a tendency to burn when I color my hair."	*"Could you please explain to me if what you've felt is a burning sensation or a tingling sensation? Many times if you shampoo your hair the same day as a color service, your scalp might tingle, since the natural oils of the scalp have just been removed. If you've felt a burning sensation, you could be experiencing an allergic reaction. In either case, please allow me to perform a patch test to ensure you're not allergic to the product."*
"I always leave the salon with a dark line on my skin."	*"I will take special precautions before the color service and apply a barrier cream to help protect your skin from staining and irritations. Also, when I shampoo the color, I can focus on trying to eliminate any dark line or shadow."*
"The color never turns out right."	*"Let's look through some magazines together to help us find out which color you like. Then I can show you a color swatch book and explain to you how I can achieve the color you want."*
"I loved the color you did last time, but it faded rather quickly and after a week, it was pretty dull already."	*"What is it you use for home care? Allow me to show you some of our color-enhancing shampoos and conditioners that will help redeposit color pigments while keeping your hair healthy and your color looking fresh between visits."*
"I'd love to change up my hair color but I don't want to get stuck having to color my hair every month because of noticeable roots."	*"There are really interesting color options with demi- or semi-permanent color products, which will fade out of your hair instead of growing out and creating a line. This allows you to change the tone or add richness to your existing color without having to deal with monthly maintenance."*

2.2 SOLID FORM

The solid form sculpture has lengths that fall to one level at the perimeter, displaying a smooth, unactivated texture. By choosing the appropriate color placement and pattern for solid form hair designs, you can emphasize the characteristics of the solid form or add the illusion of more surface activation.

SOLID FORM COLOR DESIGNING

Common color design techniques for the solid form include repetition and alternation. Repetition emphasizes the shiny appearance and the weight and volume at the form line. Alternation can create the illusion of more texture and movement. Introducing different color designs into a solid form design can dramatically change the appearance of the sculpture.

COLOR EFFECTS ON FORM

When choosing a color design with your client, one consideration that needs to be discussed is the effect that the color design should have on the form of the hair design.

Repetition of a darker color will create the look of a smooth, shiny surface, and enhance the angular shape of the solid form.

Introducing lighter colors, especially in an alternation pattern, will draw attention away from the form line and visually soften the shape.

When the hair in the exterior is colored in a contrasting color from the interior, the darker color peeks through along the form line drawing even more attention to the blunt perimeter and the concentration of weight in this area.

COLOR EFFECTS ON TEXTURE

Another aspect of a design that is affected by color is the appearance of the texture. Be sure your client understands that effect so you can make the proper choice to either enhance or visually change the textural appearance of a solid form hair design.

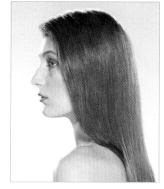

Creating a repetition of color on the solid form will cause the hair to reflect the light more evenly for a smooth, sleek appearance. This can be especially beneficial when the hair is dry and brittle or has unruly curls.

Creating an alternation of colors on the smooth surface of this design will create the illusion of additional texture. When light reflects off the hair, lighter colors will come forward, while darker colors will recede.

COLORS WITHIN SHAPES

Due to the structure of the solid form, it is not always necessary to color the entire head. Instead, the focus can be in the interior, since these lengths fall over the surface to the perimeter and an overall colored appearance is achieved.

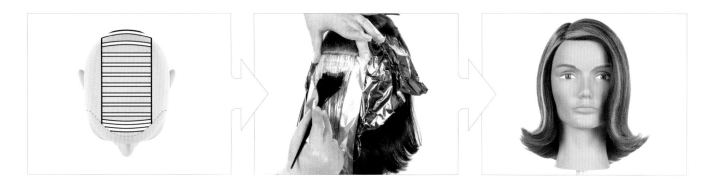

The rectangle is a popular shape used for the solid form color design. It is often positioned at the top of the head to create an alternation of colors.

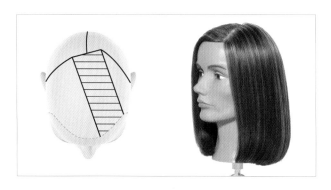

To accommodate a side part, position the rectangle on the side the hair will be parted. This will allow the highlights to fall on both sides of the part, maintaining the overall colored appearance.

WORKSHOP 01
REPETITION – VIRGIN DARKER

A repetition of color is a staple in color design that allows maximum light reflection, exhibited on the smooth surface of the solid form. An all-over color enhances the appearance of added weight, which can be ideal for clients with fine hair density.

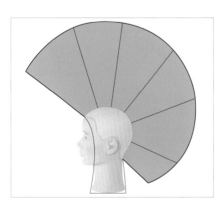

This medium field is darkened with a dark red-violet color throughout.

FORMULA: *Level 4, red-violet demi-permanent color with developer.*

This repetitious color design is created on a horizontal solid form sculpture.

Horizontal partings will be used to apply color in the back and diagonal-back partings will be used in the front.

01 Section the head into four sections from the center front hairline to the center back, and from the top of the head to each ear.

02 Apply barrier cream around the hairline and to the tops of the ears to prevent staining on the skin.

03–05 Begin by releasing a horizontal parting in the nape. Generously apply color from base to ends on top of the strands. Note that this application differs slightly from the one used in the quadrant exercise. Apply to the entire horizontal parting, working across the back section. Apply color on top of the strand and use your thumb and fingers to work the product along the strand.

06 Continue using horizontal partings as you work up the back sections. Apply the color on the top of the strands from base to ends.

07 Work across the back sections, applying the product from base to ends.

08–09 Use the same techniques as you reach the top of the section. Generously apply product from base to ends.

10 Use your thumb and fingers to work the product through the hair.

11 Carefully comb through the entire back section to ensure even application. Use a large detangling comb.

12–13 Move to the front. On one side, take a diagonal-back parting at the top and apply color on the top of the strand from base to ends. Then apply product to the bottom of the parting while laying the hair back and off the face.

14 Work downward using the same technique. At the front hairline, direct the lengths back and apply color to the bottom of the strand. Avoid applying product directly to the skin.

15 Repeat on the opposite side. When partings become too wide, subdivide for control. Continue to lay the hair away from the face as you apply to the bottom of the strands.

16 Direct the front hairline lengths back and apply color to the bottom of the strand to avoid staining the skin.

17 Outline the hairline to ensure even coverage.

18 To ensure even distribution, use a detangling comb, and carefully comb the hair away from the face.

19 Perform a strand test to check for color development.

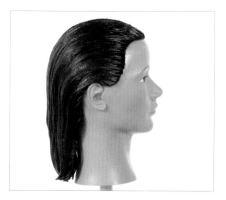

20 Process according to manufacturer's instructions. Then rinse, shampoo, condition and finish as desired.

21–22 The finish shows a repetition of deep, rich color that enhances the overall design.

REPETITION – VIRGIN DARKER

Draw or fill in the boxes with the appropriate answers.

EXISTING/DESIRED

E   E   E   E   E

D   D   D   D   D

STRUCTURE

DESIGN PRINCIPLE

☐   ☐   ☐   ☐

FORM/TEXTURE

SECTIONING/PARTING PATTERN

TOOLS/PRODUCT CHOICE

Educator Signature

Date

VARIATION 01
REPETITION – VIRGIN DARKER

In this variation, the virgin-darker technique is performed using an applicator bottle. This technique is often chosen when working with more liquid color products. Many hair designers also choose this technique as a matter of preference.

A darker copper tone is used to create a repetition of color on this uniformly layered form with a solid perimeter. The head is sectioned from the center front hairline through to the center nape and from ear to ear. Barrier cream is applied around the entire hairline. Starting at the nape, color is applied to horizontal partings from base to ends. The color is worked into the strand with the thumb. The tip of the applicator bottle can also be used. The same technique is used with horizontal partings to complete the back sections. Diagonal-back partings are used on both of the side sections. Color is applied starting at the top using the same technique, working toward the bottom and directing the hair away from the face. Then, the hair is combed through using a large-tooth comb to ensure even distribution. The color is processed according to manufacturer's instructions, rinsed, shampooed, conditioned and finished as desired.

FORMULA: *Level 6, copper demi-permanent color with developer.*

COLOR RUBRIC *WORKSHOP 01*
REPETITION – VIRGIN DARKER

This rubric is a performance assessment tool designed to measure your ability to **create** *Pivot Point color designs.*

	LEVEL 1 *in progress*	LEVEL 2 *getting better*	LEVEL 3 *entry-level proficiency*
PREPARATION			
• Assemble color design essentials	☐	☐	☐
CREATE			
• Section hair into 4 sections	☐	☐	☐
• Apply barrier cream around hairline	☐	☐	☐
• Part hair horizontally across back sections at nape	☐	☐	☐
• Apply color neatly and evenly from base to ends	☐	☐	☐
• Work upward using horizontal partings to complete back sections	☐	☐	☐
• Comb through back sections to ensure even coverage	☐	☐	☐
• Take a diagonal-back parting at top of front quadrant on one side	☐	☐	☐
• Apply color neatly and evenly from base to ends; lay hair away from face	☐	☐	☐
• Work downward using same technique, subdividing wider partings for control	☐	☐	☐
• Avoid product seepage onto skin	☐	☐	☐
• Repeat same procedure on opposite side	☐	☐	☐
• Outline hairline to ensure coverage	☐	☐	☐
• Comb hair away from face to ensure even distribution	☐	☐	☐
• Perform a strand test to check color development	☐	☐	☐
• Process color according to manufacturer's instructions	☐	☐	☐
• Rinse color from hair; shampoo and condition	☐	☐	☐
• Finish color design	☐	☐	☐

TOTAL POINTS = _____ + _____ + _____

TOTAL POINTS _____ ÷ HIGHEST POSSIBLE SCORE 54 X 100 = _____ %

Record your time in comparison with the suggested salon speed.

To improve my performance on this procedure, I need to:

_____   _____   _____
Student Signature   *Educator Signature*   *Date*

WORKSHOP 02
ALTERNATION – PARTIAL HIGHLIGHTS/ SLICING

Partial highlighting is an excellent way to break up light reflection, give the illusion of fullness and introduce the client to color services.

An alternation of pale yellow highlights is introduced to this medium-dark field, then toned with a soft, natural light blond pastel tone.

The illusion of an all-over highlighted effect can be achieved by positioning an alternation of highlights at the top area of this solid form.

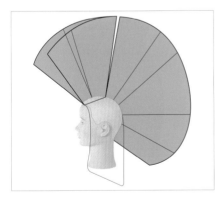

This alternation of highlights is performed on a diagonal-back solid form.

FORMULA: *Powder lightener with 20 volume (6%) developer.* TONER: *Level 9, natural blond demi-permanent color with developer.*

CREATE AS A DESIGNER

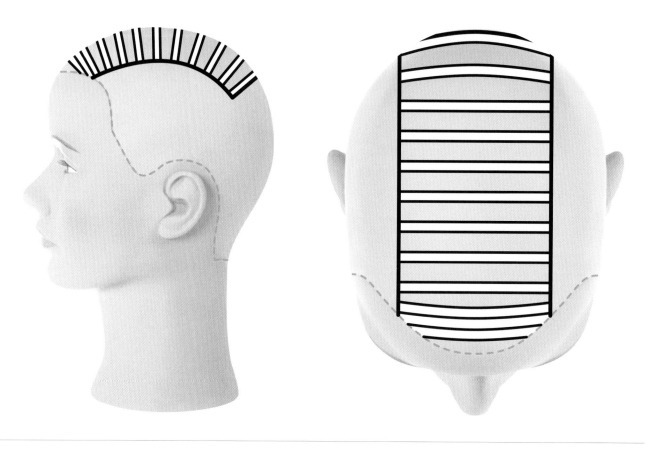

Horizontal partings are used within a rectangle shape, which extends just below the crown. The art shows that back-to-back foils will be used in the front area for a more pronounced effect.

01–03 Section the rectangle and apply barrier cream and foil to protect the untreated hair. Position the first foil at the back. Note that the silver side is used for the lightener.

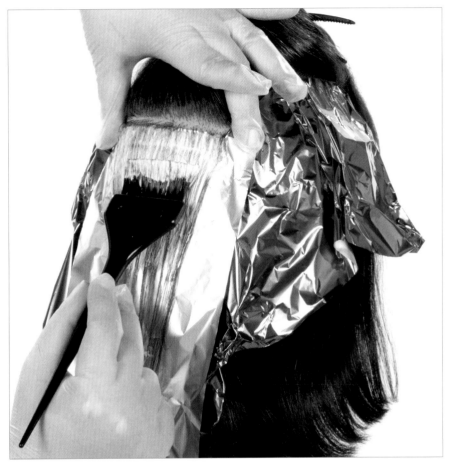

04 Take a fine slice at the crown and apply lightener to the entire strand, making sure not to exceed the edge of the foil.

05 Place another piece of foil over the lightened section.

06–07 Release the next parting, which will remain natural. Note that it is double the thickness of the highlighted section. Apply barrier cream to the base and midstrand for control. Position foil over the barrier cream. Release the next parting and apply lightener.

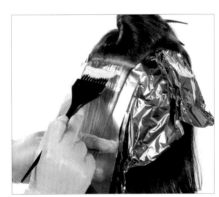

08 Continue to alternate between the highlighted and natural sections using the slicing technique. Remember to double the density of the natural hair between the highlights.

09 Apply three back-to-back foils with lightener in front for a more pronounced effect.

10–11 Leave the last section at the hairline natural, and process to the desired degree of lightness. Then remove foils, rinse and shampoo. If the desired color is achieved using lightener, condition hair and finish as desired.

12 Begin the toner application at the crown. Take a ¼" (.6 cm) horizontal parting. Use the nozzle of the bottle to distribute and apply only to the highlighted rectangle.

13 Apply toner from base to ends and use your thumb to work the product through the lengths.

14–15 Continue using horizontal partings as you work toward the front of the rectangle. Then carefully comb through the rectangle to ensure even application using a large detangling comb. Process according to manufacturer's instructions, then rinse, shampoo, condition and finish as desired.

16 Since the longest lengths of the solid form occur at the top, note how this technique creates the illusion of an overall highlighted effect.

17 When the hair is worn from a part, a bold color statement is created.

18 However, if the hair is worn away from the face, a more diffused color is achieved.

DESIGN DECISIONS *WORKSHOP 02*
ALTERNATION – PARTIAL HIGHLIGHTS/SLICING

Draw or fill in the boxes with the appropriate answers.

EXISTING/DESIRED

E   E   E   E   E

D   D   D   D   D

STRUCTURE

DESIGN PRINCIPLE

☐   ☐   ☐   ☐

FORM/TEXTURE

SECTIONING/PARTING PATTERN

TOOLS/PRODUCT CHOICE

Educator Signature

Date

BASIC COLOR DESIGN

VARIATION 02
ALTERNATION – PARTIAL HIGHLIGHTS/SLICING

In this variation, slices are used within a rectangle that is positioned diagonally to complement a side part. Slices are positioned around the perimeter to accommodate clients who prefer to wear their long lengths back off of the face or wear their hair up. These perimeter highlights can also create the illusion of added textural activation.

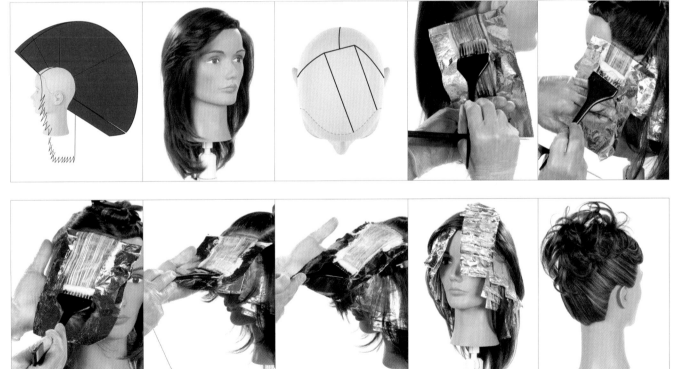

The front is sectioned with a diagonal rectangle. Diagonal partings from the top of each ear to the back corners of the rectangle are used to section the front from the back. The back is sectioned vertically at the center. Along the nape hairline, fine diagonal-back slices are taken, extending into the hairline. Slices are positioned within foils and lightener is applied from base to ends. At the sides, diagonal-back partings are used with the same slicing technique. The first slice in the rectangular shape is positioned parallel to the front hairline. Subsequent slices are positioned parallel to the first. Lightener is applied from base to ends using the same technique. The hair is lightened to the desired degree, then rinsed, shampooed, conditioned and finished as desired. When the hair is worn up or away from the face, the appearance of a full head of highlights is achieved.

FORMULA: *Highlights: lightener with 20 volume (6%) developer.* TONER: *Level 8, red-orange demi-permanent color with developer.*

COLOR RUBRIC *WORKSHOP 02*
ALTERNATION – PARTIAL HIGHLIGHTS/SLICING

This rubric is a performance assessment tool designed to measure your ability to **create** *Pivot Point color designs.*

	LEVEL 1 *in progress*	LEVEL 2 *getting better*	LEVEL 3 *entry-level proficiency*
PREPARATION			
• Assemble color design essentials	☐	☐	☐
CREATE			
• Section a rectangle shape at top of head that extends to just below crown	☐	☐	☐
• Apply barrier cream and foil to protect untreated hair along perimeter of shape	☐	☐	☐
• Position first foil at back	☐	☐	☐
• Part fine horizontal slice at crown and apply lightener to entire strand not exceeding edge of foil	☐	☐	☐
• Position another piece of foil over lightened section	☐	☐	☐
• Release next parting to be left natural; this parting should be double the density of highlighted section	☐	☐	☐
• Apply barrier cream to base and midstrand, and position foil over barrier cream	☐	☐	☐
• Release next fine slice and apply lightener	☐	☐	☐
• Alternate between fine, highlighted sections and (double density) natural sections using the slicing technique	☐	☐	☐
• Apply three back-to-back foils of lightener in front for a more pronounced effect; leave last section at front hairline natural	☐	☐	☐
• Process until desired degree of lightness is achieved	☐	☐	☐
• Remove foils, rinse, shampoo and dry	☐	☐	☐
• Part at crown using the tip of applicator bottle and ¼" (.6 cm) horizontal partings	☐	☐	☐
• Apply toner from base to ends; use thumb to work product into strand	☐	☐	☐
• Work through entire rectangle, then comb through	☐	☐	☐
• Process toner according to manufacturer's instructions	☐	☐	☐
• Rinse, shampoo and condition	☐	☐	☐
• Finish color design	☐	☐	☐

TOTAL POINTS = _____ + _____ + _____

TOTAL POINTS _____ ÷ HIGHEST POSSIBLE SCORE 57 X 100 = _____ %

Record your time in comparison with the suggested salon speed.

To improve my performance on this procedure, I need to:

_____ _____ _____

Student Signature   *Educator Signature*   *Date*

2.3 GRADUATED FORM

Because of the structure of the graduated form, the color and the sculpture need careful consideration. Color can be used to strengthen the angular shape, or downplay it to create more interest in the unactivated interior. In many cases designers choose to do both.

GRADUATED FORM COLOR DESIGNING

When the graduated form is worn in natural fall, it displays contrasting textures of activated in the exterior and unactivated in the interior, with most of the expansion along the ridgeline. Common design principles that best enhance these characteristics include contrast and alternation, or a combination of both.

COLOR EFFECTS ON FORM

Most clients who wear the graduated form love its triangular shape. Color designers will usually strive to enhance the appearance of this form. Positioning a darker color below the ridgeline will create more depth, which in turn will make the hair appear closer and "tighter" in the nape, enhancing the form. Adding lighter colors, whether in a repetition or alternation pattern above the ridgeline, will add the illusion of volume and expansion in the interior.

The repetition of a darker color throughout the nape enhances the silhouette shape.

Alternation softens the form through the interior and draws more attention to the face, while still showcasing the closeness created in the nape.

COLOR EFFECTS ON TEXTURE

Even though the graduated form has a contrast of sculpted textures, it is possible to visually transform its texture. The placement of each color needs to be determined by considering the position of the ridgeline within the sculpture. To reduce the texture activation in the exterior, a repetition of a darker color can be applied below the ridgeline. To create more activation in the interior, an alternation of colors can be applied above the ridgeline. Another option is to create a "veiled" effect. This positions the lighter color just underneath the surface lengths, adding excitement and dimension.

A repetition of color will create maximum light reflection, which results in a smooth appearance.

Alternation of color will create textural interest and activation through the otherwise unactivated surface lengths.

Veiled alternation will add excitement and dimension by peeking through the top lengths of the hair.

COLORS WITHIN SHAPES

A common shape used with the graduated form is the triangle. Triangular sections can vary in size, shape and position as shown in the examples below.

A triangle positioned at the front hairline will create more interest and volume around the face. An alternation of highlights within this triangle will create added texture within the unactivated lengths and diminish toward the back.

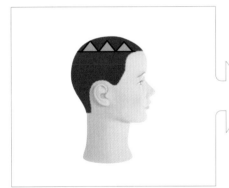  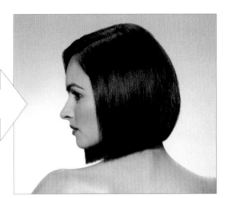

Another way to use triangles is to position them underneath the top layer of the hair. Styling the hair will allow the colored hair to be more or less visible.

WORKSHOP 03
CONTRAST – TRIANGLES

A versatile color effect is the result of designing color that can either be hidden or revealed by the longer lengths of this graduated form. Bold color placement underneath a smooth surface offers the client various color effects, depending on how the hair is finished.

Triangular shapes are prelightened and then a red-orange color is applied throughout this medium field.

The finish allows more or less of the bold color to show depending on how the hair is styled.

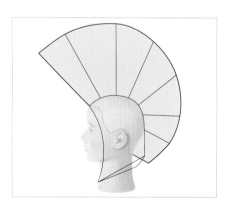

This contrast of color is created on a graduated sculpture.

FORMULA: *On-the-scalp lightener with 20 volume (6%) developer.* TONER: *Level 7, red-orange demi-permanent color with developer.*

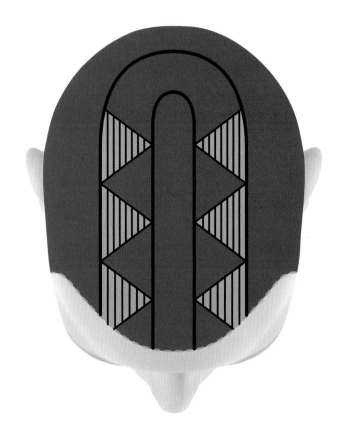
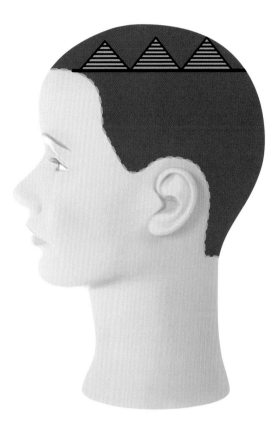

Two horseshoe-shaped partings are used to section the interior. The outer parting at the crest is used to section the lengths that will not be treated during the first part of the application. The inner section at the center top will act as a veil that falls over the lightened triangles. The triangles are sectioned between these two lines, on either side of the inner section, with the narrow end toward the center. Horizontal partings will be used to apply lightener to the triangles.

01–02 Use a horseshoe-shaped parting to create a narrow section at the center top. Use another horseshoe-shaped parting at the crest to determine the depth of the triangles and isolate the exterior. Apply barrier cream and thermal strips to protect the untreated hair beneath these sections.

03 Use a large zigzag parting to create three triangle-shaped sections on either side of the center section.

04 Begin on the right side and secure the remainder of the hair to the opposite side.

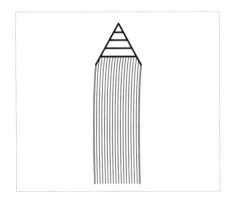

05 Start at the front triangle by taking a ⅛" (.3 cm) horizontal parting at the bottom of the triangle. Place a longer thermal strip below the triangle, then apply lightener from the base to the ends. Carefully work to the top of the triangle. Use the same techniques to apply to the next triangle.

06–07 Cover each triangle with two thermal strips to ensure coverage. Place a short thermal strip vertically at the bottom of the treated hair. Then use a longer strip diagonally, lining up the edge of the strip with the edge of the triangle. If necessary, fold the edge of the thermal strip to fit the triangle.

08 Complete the third triangle on this side using the same techniques.

09 Repeat these techniques on the other side.

10–11 Process until the desired degree of lightness is achieved. Rinse, shampoo and dry the hair in preparation for the toner application.

NOTE: *You may condition and finish the design now if the desired contrasting color effect is achieved.*

12 After applying barrier cream, apply the toner from base to ends. Process according to manufacturer's instructions, checking the color as necessary. Then rinse, shampoo, condition and finish as desired.

13–14 The exposure of color can range from subtle to dramatic, bold or diffused, depending on the placement of triangles, the direction the hair is styled and the color chosen.

DESIGN DECISIONS *WORKSHOP 03*
CONTRAST – TRIANGLES
Draw or fill in the boxes with the appropriate answers.

EXISTING/DESIRED

E   E   E   E   E

D   D   D   D   D

STRUCTURE

DESIGN PRINCIPLE

☐   ☐   ☐   ☐

FORM/TEXTURE

SECTIONING/PARTING PATTERN

TOOLS/PRODUCT CHOICE

Educator Signature   *Date*

COLOR RUBRIC *WORKSHOP 03*
CONTRAST – TRIANGLES

This rubric is a performance assessment tool designed to measure your ability to ***create*** *Pivot Point color designs.*

	LEVEL 1 *in progress*	LEVEL 2 *getting better*	LEVEL 3 *entry-level proficiency*
PREPARATION			
• Assemble color design essentials	☐	☐	☐
CREATE			
• Section a narrow horseshoe shape at top	☐	☐	☐
• Section another horseshoe-shaped parting at crest determining depth of triangles and isolating exterior	☐	☐	☐
• Apply barrier cream and thermal strips to protect untreated hair beneath section	☐	☐	☐
• Section three triangle shapes using large zigzag partings on either side of center section; secure remainder of hair to opposite side	☐	☐	☐
• Part front triangle using ⅛" (.3 cm) horizontal partings to ensure even application of lightener	☐	☐	☐
• Place longer thermal strip under first parting	☐	☐	☐
• Apply lightener from base to ends	☐	☐	☐
• Repeat same parting and application method until entire triangle is saturated	☐	☐	☐
• Position two thermal strips over saturated triangle section to ensure coverage; line up top strip diagonally to corner of triangle, folding if necessary	☐	☐	☐
• Repeat same application technique in the other two triangles, covering each triangle with two thermal strips	☐	☐	☐
• Repeat same techniques on opposite side	☐	☐	☐
• Process until desired degree of lightness is achieved	☐	☐	☐
• Rinse lightener, shampoo and dry hair	☐	☐	☐
• Place barrier cream around hairline	☐	☐	☐
• Apply toner from base to ends	☐	☐	☐
• Process color according to manufacturer's instructions	☐	☐	☐
• Rinse, shampoo and condition hair	☐	☐	☐
• Finish color design	☐	☐	☐

TOTAL POINTS = _____ + _____ + _____

TOTAL POINTS _____ ÷ HIGHEST POSSIBLE SCORE 57 X 100 = _____ %

Record your time in comparison with the suggested salon speed.

To improve my performance on this procedure, I need to:

_____ _____ _____
Student Signature   Educator Signature   Date

WORKSHOP 04
CONTRAST – HIGHLIGHTS/ ZONES/WEAVING

This highlighting technique will position highlights away from the scalp using zigzag partings. This avoids creating a strong line of demarcation. The exterior is colored darker to create the illusion of a more contoured effect. The addition of this bolder color pattern on a classic design creates a dramatic frame for the face.

An alternation of highlights is positioned within a triangle at the fringe, while a darker color in the exterior is added to this medium dark field.

This alternation of color is created on a graduated form.

FORMULA: *Exterior: Level 6, gold permanent color with 20 volume (6%) developer. Interior: Lightener with 20 volume (6%) developer.*
TONER: *Level 8, gold demi-permanent color with developer.*

01 Begin by sectioning a triangle at the fringe. Section the interior from the exterior. Clip the middle section up and out of the way.

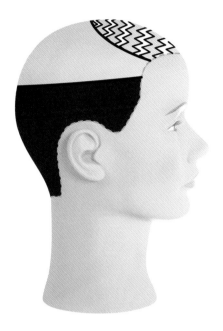

02 Apply barrier cream around the hairline to protect the skin and prevent staining.

The hair is sectioned with a slightly diagonal-back line at the crest. While many patterns can be used, horizontal partings are used in the back, while diagonal-back partings are used at the sides to apply color in the exterior. Diagonal zigzag partings will be used for the top triangle to create chunky alternation highlights in the fringe.

03–04 Section the back in half vertically and part horizontally starting in the nape. Apply the darker color from base to ends using the virgin-darker technique. Start at the center and work toward each side. Work upward.

05 At the sides, take diagonal partings and direct the hair away from the face. Apply product from base to ends using the virgin-darker technique.

06 Position a thermal strip over the area that has been colored. This will protect the uncolored hair from being stained.

07–08 Move to the fringe section. Leave the front hairline natural. Position a zigzag parting diagonally, approximately ½" (1.25 cm) thick. Note that both the top and bottom of the parting are zigzagged.

10 Apply lightener away from the base of the foil.

11 Continue applying lightener to the remainder of the strand.

09 Position foil underneath the section of hair. Due to the size and depth of the zigzag parting, the base of the foil rests farther away from the top of the parting. The steeper the zigzag, the farther away the foil will be.

12 Position the brush at an angle and blend the product at the base. This will allow for a more diffused line of color.

13–14 Fold the foil upward and use the teeth of the tail comb to crease and fold the sides of the foil toward the center.

16 Apply product from the edge of the foil to the ends of the hair.

17 Use the same technique to fold the foil.

15 Work toward the back of the section, making each subsequent zigzag parting thinner. Continue to apply the lightener for an irregular effect at the base. Position the brush at an angle while applying the product to the edge of the foil.

18 Create increasingly thinner zigzag partings as you work toward the back of this section, applying lightener from the edge of the foil to the ends.

19 Process until the desired degree of lightness is achieved. Remove the foils and thermal strips, then rinse, shampoo and dry the hair.

20 Apply the toner to the entire head. Process according to manufacturer's instructions then rinse, shampoo, condition and finish the hair as desired.

21 This technique positions highlights away from the scalp, eliminating a line of demarcation.

22 Keep in mind that the color chosen for the exterior can affect the overall feeling of the design, creating more or less contrast with the highlighted fringe. Here a warm, natural overall effect is achieved while adding textural interest in the design.

DESIGN DECISIONS *WORKSHOP 04*
CONTRAST – HIGHLIGHTS/ZONES/WEAVING

artist+
access.

Draw or fill in the boxes with the appropriate answers.

EXISTING/DESIRED

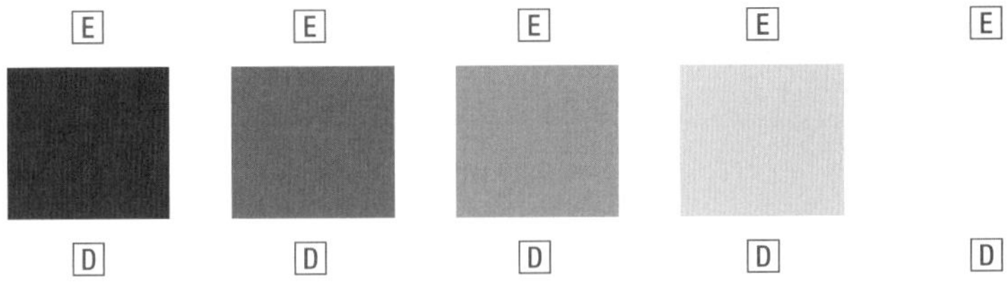

E   E   E   E   E

D   D   D   D   D

STRUCTURE

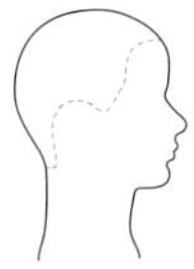

DESIGN PRINCIPLE

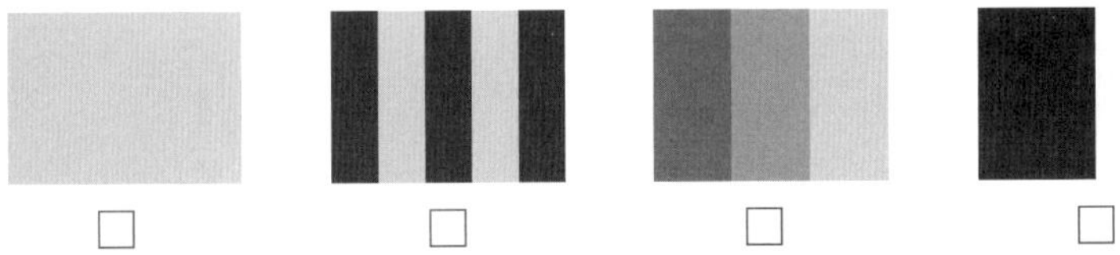

☐   ☐   ☐   ☐

FORM/TEXTURE

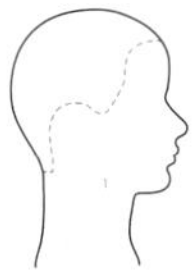

SECTIONING/PARTING PATTERN

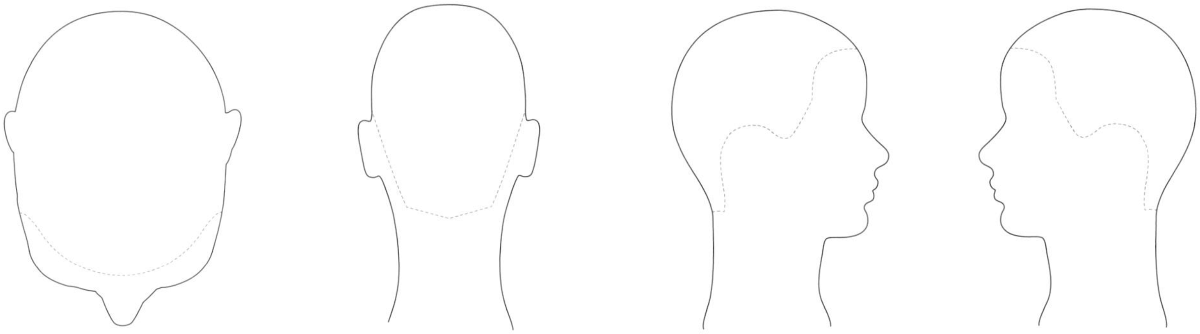

TOOLS/PRODUCT CHOICE

Educator Signature

Date

CONTRAST – HIGHLIGHTS/ ZONES/WEAVING

A shape within a shape can be used when a progression of highlights is desired with more highlights in one area and fewer highlights in another area. Here, a smaller triangle is positioned within a larger triangle in the interior to create more highlights near the face. The proportion of each triangle and the techniques used within can vary according to the desired results.

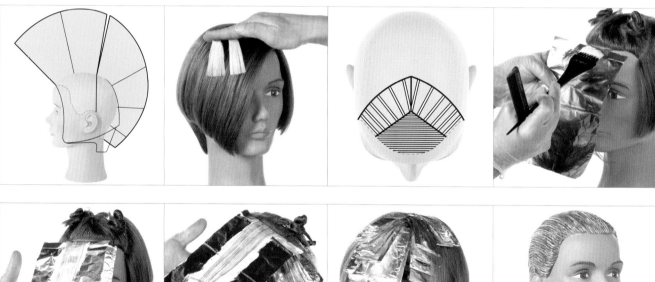

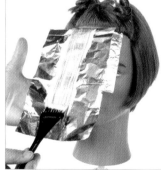

A triangle is positioned at the center front hairline within a wider triangle from the apex to the recession area on either side. The outer shape is subsectioned with a center parting. Within the smaller triangle, thin horizontal partings and fine slices are taken, starting at the front hairline. Slices are positioned within foils and lightener is applied from base to ends. Foils are folded upward with the sides folded toward the center. Wider slices are subdivided for added control. At the sides, diagonal-back partings are used to create fine slices with more untreated hair between the slices than in the front triangle. Product is applied from base to ends and foils are folded using the same technique. Toward the back of these sections, slices are adapted to gradually become more parallel to the center sectioning line. After the lightener processes, the hair is rinsed, shampooed and dried before a light violet-based toner is applied.

FORMULA: *Lightener with 20 volume (6%) developer.* TONER: *Level 10, violet demi-permanent color with developer.*

COLOR RUBRIC *WORKSHOP 04*
CONTRAST – HIGHLIGHTS/ZONES/WEAVING

This rubric is a performance assessment tool designed to measure your ability to *create* Pivot Point color designs.

	LEVEL 1 *in progress*	LEVEL 2 *getting better*	LEVEL 3 *entry-level proficiency*
PREPARATION			
• Assemble color design essentials	☐	☐	☐
CREATE			
• Section a triangle at fringe, secure	☐	☐	☐
• Section crest area following diagonal-back ridgeline, secure	☐	☐	☐
• Apply barrier cream along hairline	☐	☐	☐
• Section back in center for control	☐	☐	☐
• Part horizontally across both sections beginning at hairline in nape	☐	☐	☐
• Apply darker color from base to ends using virgin-darker technique	☐	☐	☐
• Apply using diagonal-back partings at sides	☐	☐	☐
• Position thermal strip to cover colored hair	☐	☐	☐
• Release triangle section in fringe; leave front hairline natural	☐	☐	☐
• Release ½" (1.25 cm) thick diagonal parting, zigzagged on both sides	☐	☐	☐
• Position foil underneath section	☐	☐	☐
• Apply lightener away from base of foil, then to remainder of strand	☐	☐	☐
• Position brush at angle, blend lightener at base	☐	☐	☐
• Fold foil upward and fold sides of foil toward center with tail comb	☐	☐	☐
• Leave untreated hair between foils	☐	☐	☐
• Take increasingly thinner partings while working toward back	☐	☐	☐
• Apply product using same procedures for an irregular effect at base; fold foil using same technique	☐	☐	☐
• Work to back of triangle	☐	☐	☐
• Process until desired degree of lightness is achieved	☐	☐	☐
• Remove foils and thermal strips, rinse color, shampoo and dry hair	☐	☐	☐
• Apply toner to entire head from base to ends	☐	☐	☐
• Rinse, shampoo and condition	☐	☐	☐
• Finish color design	☐	☐	☐

TOTAL POINTS = _____ + _____ + _____

TOTAL POINTS _____ ÷ HIGHEST POSSIBLE SCORE 72 X 100 = _____ %

Record your time in comparison with the suggested salon speed. _____

To improve my performance on this procedure, I need to: _____

_____   _____   _____
Student Signature   *Educator Signature*   *Date*

2.4 INCREASE-LAYERED FORM

The increase-layered form allows clients to maintain their long lengths while achieving great activated texture. Choosing the proper color placement and coloring techniques can enhance the activated texture and make the form line appear fuller.

INCREASE-LAYERED FORM COLOR DESIGNING

Common design principles used for increase-layered form color designs include progression and alternation. Introducing color into a sculpture can dramatically change the appearance of the increase-layered form design.

COLOR EFFECTS ON FORM

Many people choose an increase-layered sculpture because they want long hair and also like shorter lengths in the interior to style for volume. Color can often be used to help accentuate these aspects of the form.

Creating increase layers on a client with fine hair might cause the perimeter to look thin and transparent. By applying a deeper, richer color to the longest lengths, the form line will appear thicker and more dense. Adding lighter colors to the interior will create the illusion of more volume.

COLOR EFFECTS ON TEXTURE

Depending on the client's hair texture, density or preference, designers can choose to either enhance the activated texture of the increase-layered form or diminish its textured appearance.

Placing a contrasting color along shorter increase-layered strands along the face accentuates where the activated texture falls.

With an activated surface texture and activated sculpted lengths, a progression of color with maximum blending will soften the texture and calm the eye.

An alternation of color will create added textural interest and volume.

COLORS WITHIN SHAPES

Zonal patterns that involve circles or ovals are commonly used to create a progression of color. The lines between zones can either be straight or zigzag.

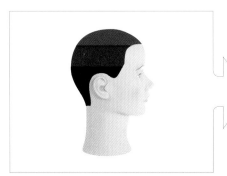  

Straight sectioning lines allow the transition to be more noticeable.

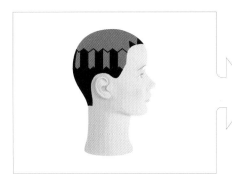  

When using zigzag sectioning lines, the transition between colors will be the softest.

WORKSHOP 05
PROGRESSION – ZONES

Zonal patterns are commonly used to create a progression of colors. Playing with color tonal variations within zones can create a transitional blending and progression of tones. It can also create an illusion of added fullness and depth depending on zone placement and color choices.

Three rich, reddish colors are introduced to this medium field to create a soft, harmonious tonal change with depth and dimension.

This progression is created on a diagonal-forward, increase-layered form sculpture.

FORMULA: *Lower Zone: Level 5, violet brown permanent color with 20 volume (6%) developer; Middle Zone: Level 6, red permanent color with 20 volume (6%) developer; Upper Zone: Level 7, red copper permanent color with 30 volume (9%) developer.*

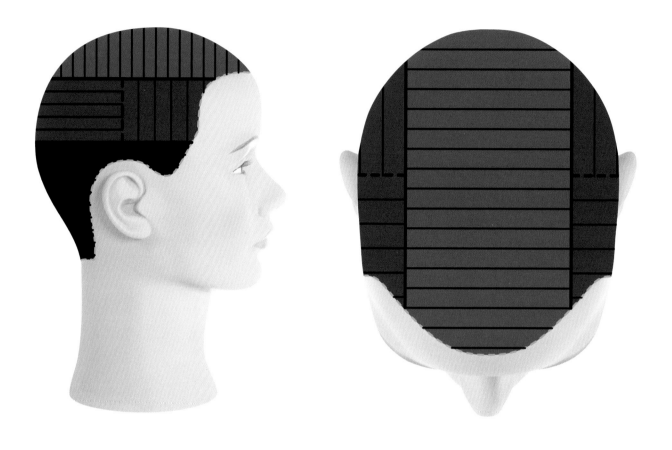

The art shows three zones sectioned horizontally around the curve of the head. Horizontal partings will be used to apply color in the lower and upper zones. In the middle zone, a combination of horizontal partings in back and vertical partings at the sides will be used.

01 Begin by sectioning the head horizontally into three zones. The middle zone is subsectioned vertically at the center back for control.

02 Apply barrier cream around the hairline to prevent staining on the skin.

03 Begin the application at the center nape. Use horizontal partings to apply the darkest, coolest color from base to ends.

04 Apply color on top of the strand and use your thumb to work the product in along the strand.

05 Extend the horizontal partings to the sides and apply color from base to ends. Direct the hair back and away from the face.

06 When the application to the perimeter zone is complete, position long thermal strips to isolate the section.

07 Next, subdivide the middle zone vertically above each ear. Begin applying the middle color at the center back using horizontal partings to work across the back section.

08 Apply from base to ends and use your thumb to work the product in along the hair strand. Work to the top of this section.

09 At the sides of the middle zone, use vertical partings. Apply the color from base to ends, directing the hair back and away from the face as you apply. Work to the front of one side, then repeat on the opposite side.

10 Then position long thermal strips to isolate the middle zone.

11–12 Next, apply the lightest color to the top zone. Use horizontal partings and apply from base to ends. Work from the crown to the front hairline. Check and outline the hairline to ensure even coverage.

13 Process according to manufacturer's instructions. Then rinse, shampoo, condition and finish as desired.

14–15 The finish shows rich colors, which create a soft, harmonious progression from deeper, cooler tones in the exterior to lighter, warmer tones in the interior.

PROGRESSION – ZONES
Draw or fill in the boxes with the appropriate answers.

artist⁺
access.

EXISTING/DESIRED

E   E   E   E   E

D   D   D   D   D

STRUCTURE

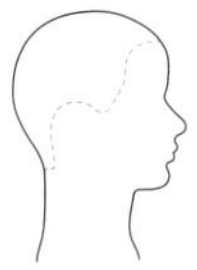

DESIGN PRINCIPLE

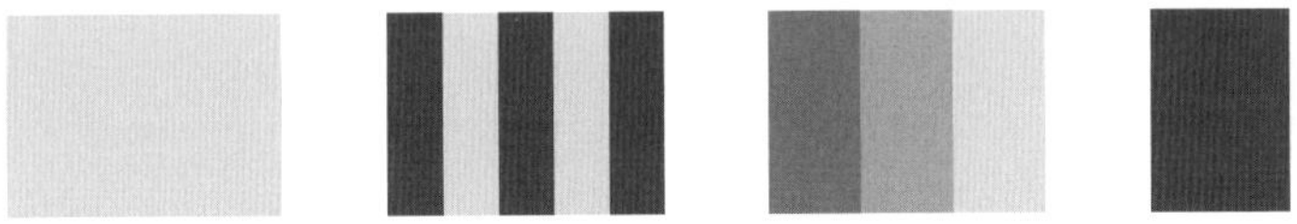

☐   ☐   ☐   ☐

FORM/TEXTURE

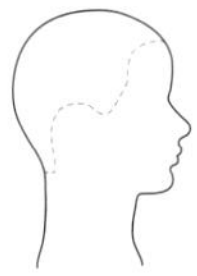

SECTIONING/PARTING PATTERN

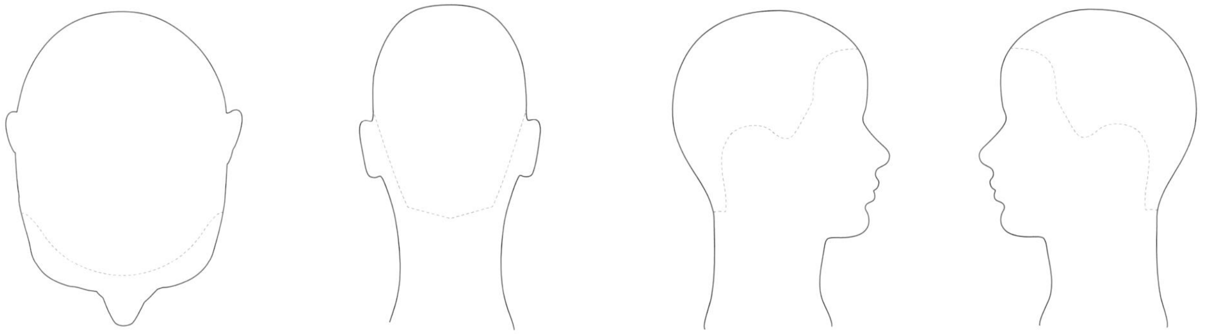

TOOLS/PRODUCT CHOICE

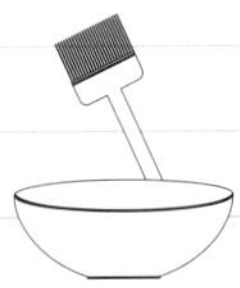

Educator Signature

Date

VARIATION 04
PROGRESSION – ZONES

Smaller shapes can be used within a zone to create a transition between two other zones. In this variation, an alternation of the lighter and darker colors in the middle zone allows for maximum blending between the interior and exterior. This can be especially effective for clients with curly hair. In this design, a darker color is applied to the nape while a lighter color is applied to the top. These colors are then alternated in the middle zone to create a transitional blend and a progression of tones.

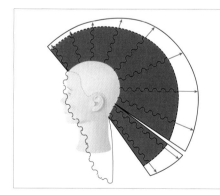

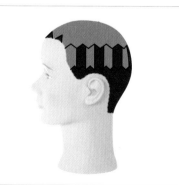

Darker and lighter red tones are used to create a color progression on this increase-layered form. Zigzag partings are used to divide the head into three zones. Small triangles are also isolated at the front hairline. The middle zone is then subdivided with vertical partings to create an odd number of subsections. Note that the odd number of sections creates a symmetric alternation on either side of the center back.

FORMULA: *Exterior: Level 4, red-violet permanent color with 10 volume (3%) developer; Interior: Level 6, copper red permanent color with 20 volume (6%) developer.*

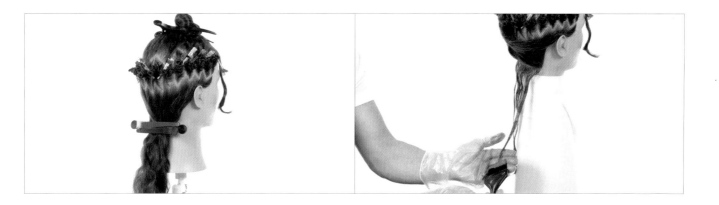

The application starts in the nape, where a darker red color is applied to horizontal partings from base to ends. At the zigzag parting, the brush is angled to accommodate the partings. Foil is positioned over the color in this zone and every other subsection is released in the midzone. The same color used in the nape is applied from base to ends to the hair that is released. Then the remaining subsections are released and a lighter red is applied from base to ends. Foil is then positioned over the middle zone. The lighter red color is then applied from base to ends in the interior zone using horizontal partings, starting in the back. The application continues toward the front hairline, excluding the small triangles. Foil is positioned over the last zone and the darker color is applied to the triangular shapes. The color is processed according to manufacturer's instructions, then rinsed, shampooed, conditioned and finished as desired.

COLOR RUBRIC *WORKSHOP 05*
PROGRESSION – ZONES

This rubric is a performance assessment tool designed to measure your ability to create Pivot Point color designs.

	LEVEL 1 *in progress*	LEVEL 2 *getting better*	LEVEL 3 *entry-level proficiency*
PREPARATION			
• Assemble color design essentials	☐	☐	☐
CREATE			
• Section head into 3 zones	☐	☐	☐
• Subdivide hair vertically in the middle zone	☐	☐	☐
• Apply barrier cream around hairline	☐	☐	☐
• Apply darkest (cool) color from base to ends in nape section using horizontal partings	☐	☐	☐
• Extend horizontal partings to sides and direct hair back from face	☐	☐	☐
• Position long thermal strips over color when zone is complete	☐	☐	☐
• Subdivide middle zone above each ear	☐	☐	☐
• Release horizontal parting across back middle section and apply middle color from base to ends	☐	☐	☐
• Part vertically at sides of middle zone and apply lighter color from base to ends, directing hair away from face	☐	☐	☐
• Position long thermal strips over color when zone is complete	☐	☐	☐
• Take horizontal partings in top zone and apply lightest (warm) color from base to ends	☐	☐	☐
• Work from crown toward front hairline	☐	☐	☐
• Process color according to manufacturer's instructions	☐	☐	☐
• Rinse, shampoo and condition	☐	☐	☐
• Finish color design	☐	☐	☐

TOTAL POINTS = _____ + _____ + _____

TOTAL POINTS _____ ÷ HIGHEST POSSIBLE SCORE 48 X 100 = _____ %

Record your time in comparison with the suggested salon speed.

To improve my performance on this procedure, I need to:

_____
Student Signature

_____
Educator Signature

_____
Date

WORKSHOP 06
PROGRESSION – HIGHLIGHTS/ WEAVING

A color progression from a lighter crown to a darker perimeter can enhance light reflection on a layered form and create the illusion of more volume in the crown. At the same time, darker perimeter tones frame the face. Creating this progression using a highlight-weaving technique also visually enhances texture activation. The palette comb is a quick and effective alternative to foiling, used to create highlights and/ or lowlights within a color design.

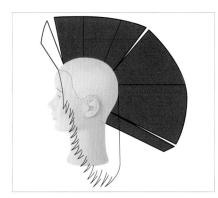

Fine and medium-woven sections are used to create a progression to the deeper-colored perimeter. A violet-based toner is applied to the entire design for a harmonizing effect. The result subtly enhances the shape and activated texture of the form.

This progression of color was performed on a planar/conversion, increase-layered form.

FORMULA: *Powder lightener with 20 volume (6%) developer.* TONER: *Level 8, violet demi-permanent color with developer.*

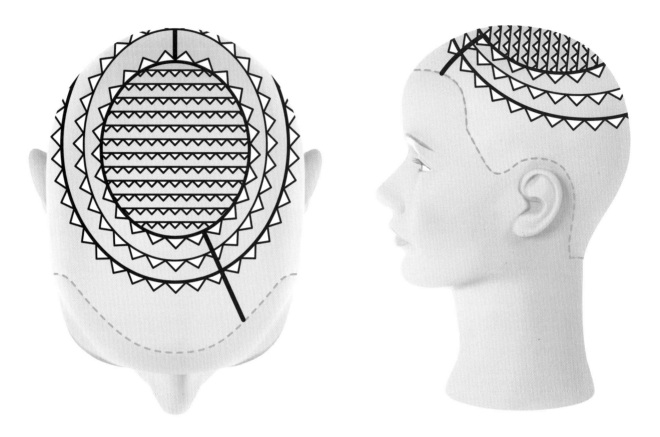

The art shows that the head is sectioned into three zones: perimeter, middle and crown. The circular crown section is surrounded by another curved section, the middle zone, which is slightly narrower at the front and wider at the back. Medium-woven partings will be used in the middle zone and fine, horizontal-woven partings will be used in the crown. The perimeter zone will be left natural during the first application. A side part extends from the front hairline through the middle zone, which is also sub-sectioned at the center back for control.

01 Section the head into three zones.

02–03 Use the outside sectioning line of the middle zone to begin. Part off a medium-thick parting and use a tail comb to create a medium weave. Position the palette comb under the woven strands and apply lightener to the hair starting near the base. Move the palette comb slowly along the strands as you continue to apply the lightener. Work to the ends and gently lay the hair down.

04 Continue to use a medium weave and the palette comb technique as you work toward the center back.

05 Move to the other side and use the same technique, working from the side part to the center back.

06 Next, divide the middle zone in half and use the medium-weaving technique. Use the same technique to apply lightener.

07 The sectioning line around the crown will be used to weave the last portion of the middle zone.

08 Release the remaining hair in the middle zone. Use the sectioning line around the crown and the same medium-weaving technique. Work from the front to the center back on either side.

09 Move to the crown and release a thin horizontal parting at the back of the section. Use a fine-weaving technique, then position the palette comb parallel to the parting at the base. The use of fine partings and weaves will create a heavier density of highlights.

10 Use the same technique to apply lightener from base to ends. Gently lay the hair down. Work toward the front, subdividing wider partings for control.

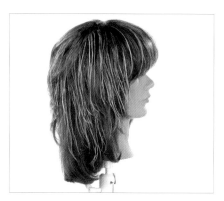

11–12 The completed application shows a heavier density of highlights applied within the top crown zone than the middle zone. Process until the desired degree of lightness is achieved. Rinse thoroughly, shampoo and dry.

13 Apply toner from base to ends. Process according to manufacturer's instructions. Then, rinse, shampoo, condition and style as desired.

14–15 The finish shows a progression from the lighter crown to darker perimeter lengths, creating a subtle illusion of additional volume and texture.

DESIGN DECISIONS *WORKSHOP 06*
PROGRESSION – HIGHLIGHTS/WEAVING

artist⁺ access.

Draw or fill in the boxes with the appropriate answers.

EXISTING/DESIRED

E   E   E   E   E

D   D   D   D   D

STRUCTURE

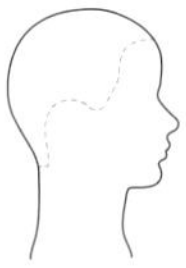

DESIGN PRINCIPLE

FORM/TEXTURE

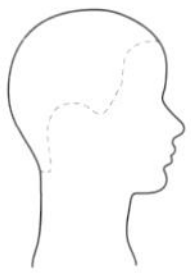

SECTIONING/PARTING PATTERN

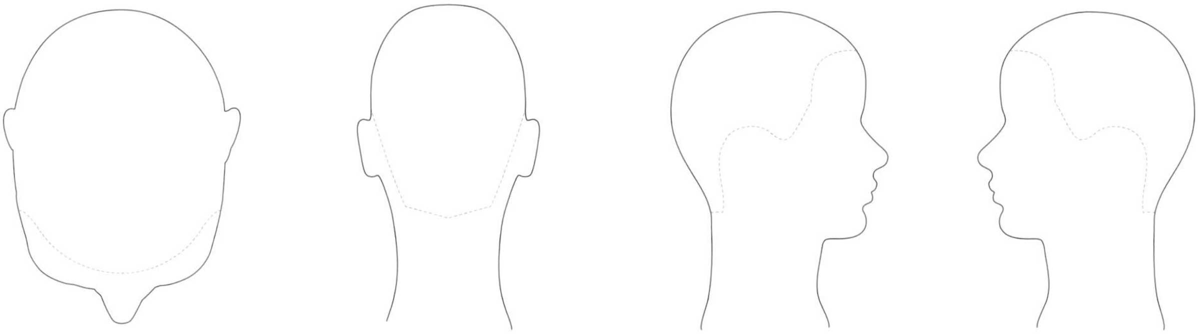

TOOLS/PRODUCT CHOICE

_____   _____

Educator Signature   *Date*

COLOR RUBRIC *WORKSHOP 06*
PROGRESSION – HIGHLIGHTS/WEAVING

This rubric is a performance assessment tool designed to measure your ability to
create Pivot Point color designs.

	LEVEL 1 *in progress*	LEVEL 2 *getting better*	LEVEL 3 *entry-level proficiency*
PREPARATION			
• Assemble color design essentials	☐	☐	☐
CREATE			
• Section head into 3 zones	☐	☐	☐
• Section a circular zone at crown surrounded by another curved section, narrower in front and wider in back	☐	☐	☐
• Subdivide middle zone at side part and center back	☐	☐	☐
• Part medium parting and use tail comb to create medium weave; begin at front outside sectioning line of middle zone	☐	☐	☐
• Position palette comb under woven strands near base	☐	☐	☐
• Apply lightener to hair moving palette comb along hair strand slowly	☐	☐	☐
• Work toward center back using same procedures	☐	☐	☐
• Work from side part to back on opposite side using same procedures	☐	☐	☐
• Divide middle zone in half parallel to sectioning line	☐	☐	☐
• Use medium-weaving technique with palette comb; work from side part to center back on both sides	☐	☐	☐
• Release remainder of middle zone	☐	☐	☐
• Use sectioning line around crown and same techniques to weave and apply lightener from front to center back on either side	☐	☐	☐
• Release thin horizontal parting in back of crown zone	☐	☐	☐
• Apply lightener using fine-weaving technique and palette comb	☐	☐	☐
• Repeat same procedure working toward front of crown zone	☐	☐	☐
• Subdivide wider partings for control	☐	☐	☐
• Process until desired degree of lightness is achieved	☐	☐	☐
• Rinse, shampoo and dry hair	☐	☐	☐
• Apply toner from base to ends	☐	☐	☐
• Process according to manufacturer's instructions	☐	☐	☐
• Rinse, shampoo and condition hair	☐	☐	☐
• Finish color design	☐	☐	☐

TOTAL POINTS = _____ + _____ + _____

TOTAL POINTS _____ ÷ HIGHEST POSSIBLE SCORE 69 X 100 = _____ %

Record your time in comparison with the suggested salon speed.

To improve my performance on this procedure, I need to:

_____   _____   _____
Student Signature   *Educator Signature*   *Date*

2.5 UNIFORMLY LAYERED FORM

Color options are endless for a uniformly layered hair sculpture. After looking at some of the ways in which this form can be colored, you will see how much you can emphasize or alter the appearance of the form or the texture depending on the desired results.

UNIFORMLY LAYERED FORM COLOR DESIGNING

There are many color options available for the uniformly layered form. The most popular choices include repetition and alternation, but progression and contrast can also be effective. Introducing color into this sculpture can dramatically change its appearance.

COLOR EFFECTS ON FORM

Since the uniformly layered form has consistent lengths throughout the design and often resembles a circle, color considerations include deciding whether you wish to enhance the rounded shape or visually change the form. An alternation of color would minimize the form and draw attention away from the shape.

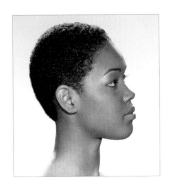

Applying a repetition of color draws attention to and enhances the shape of the form.

Coloring just the exterior darker will make the form appear narrower and closer in the nape, allowing the shape to resemble a graduated form.

COLOR EFFECTS ON TEXTURE

The texture of the uniformly layered form is highly activated. This can, however, sometimes be too much of a good thing, especially on curly hair that is uniformly layered.

Selecting an alternation of color will create the illusion of additional activation, which can be a great design choice.

Calmer color patterns such as overall repetition will help neutralize the totally activated texture, especially when darker color shades are used.

COLORS WITHIN SHAPES

With so many styling options available, almost any shape can be used to design color for this form.

The circle allows you to achieve a similar color pattern no matter how the hair is styled.

WORKSHOP 07
ALTERNATION – HIGHLIGHTS/ LOWLIGHTS/ WEAVING

Alternating a lighter and darker color in a design is a great way to create an interesting color change. This type of color design adds depth and dimension and is especially complementary for layered textures.

Highlights and lowlights are alternated throughout this medium field. A violet-based toner is then applied over the entire head.

The finish shows a multi-dimensional color effect that enhances the texture of the form.

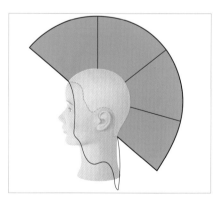

This alternation of a lighter and darker color is created on a uniformly layered form.

FORMULA: *Highlights: Powder lightener with 20 volume (6%) developer; Lowlights: Level 5, gold permanent color with 10 volume (3%) developer.*
TONER: *Level 8, violet demi-permanent with developer.*

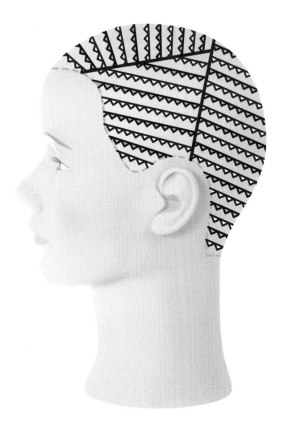

The art shows the head sectioned diagonally from ear to ear over the crown. The front is further sectioned with a center rectangle through the top and the back is sectioned with a vertical line at the center back. Medium weaves will be used along shallow diagonal-back partings at the back. Diagonal-back partings at the sides are slightly adapted toward the top to accommodate the shape of the section and horizontal partings will be used in the top section.

01 Section the head into five sections.

02–03 Begin on the right side of the nape. Release a shallow diagonal-back parting in the right nape section. Then create a medium weave using the end of the tail comb. Position the foil at the scalp under the woven strands.

04 Apply the lightener to the hair from the edge of the foil to the ends.

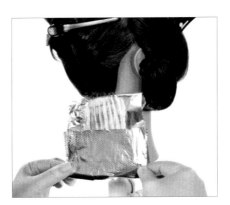

05–06 Use the double-fold technique, folding the foil approximately ⅓ upward, then folding up to the parting.

07 Place the tail of the comb under the foil to reinforce its position close to the scalp. Then use the comb to crease and fold each side toward the center.

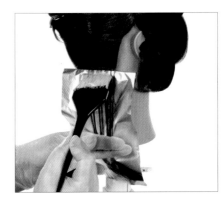

08 Release the next diagonal parting, repeat the same weaving technique and apply the darker color from base to ends. Use a different color foil to identify the darker color.

09 Use the same technique to fold the foil.

10 Work toward the top, alternating highlights and lowlights. As partings become too wide, subsection and apply two foils to allow more control and proper color development. Note that you may need to subsection more than once in the widest area.

11 Weave, foil and apply color onto one section and then the other. Foil both sections evenly to avoid overlapping. Note that foils should be placed next to each other.

12 Reinforce the foil to prevent product seepage.

13–14 As you reach the top, continue to alternate the lightener and darker color. Use the same weaving and foiling techniques to complete the section.

15 Next, move to the left side of the nape. Apply lightener to the first parting to match the color sequence on the right side.

16–17 As you work up this section, maintain consistent diagonal-back partings and subsection to encompass the wider areas.

19 Position the foil and apply lightener. Then fold the foil using the same technique used in the back.

18 Move to one side and release a diagonal-back parting at the bottom of the section. Weave the top strands to be consistent with the woven strands in the back sections.

20 As you work upward, alternating the lightener and darker color, subsection at the widest area.

21 As you work toward the top, slightly adapt the angle of the partings to become less diagonal. Note that the last part and weave are parallel to the top sectioning line.

22 Move to the other side and repeat the same weaving and foiling techniques using the same partings. Again, apply the lightener to the first parting, then alternate as you work toward the top.

23 Next, move to the center panel. Release a horizontal parting at the front hairline. Use the tail of the comb to weave the top strands, creating a medium weave. Lightener will be applied to the first parting in this section also.

24 Apply lightener from the edge of the foil to the ends. Fold the foil using the same technique used at the back and sides.

25 Repeat the same weaving and foiling techniques in the next parting. Apply the darker color and use the darker foil.

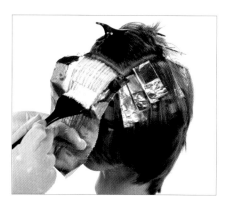

26 Continue to alternate between lightener and the darker color as you work toward the back of the section.

27 Maintain even partings and use consistent medium weaves.

28–29 The completed application shows an alternation of light and dark foils from horizontal and diagonal-back partings. Allow the lightener and color to develop according to the manufacturer's instructions. Rinse thoroughly, shampoo, then dry the hair. Do not condition the hair at this point.

30 Apply toner to the entire head from base to ends. Process according to the manufacturer's instructions. Then rinse, shampoo, condition and finish as desired.

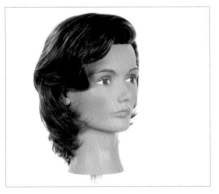

31–32 The finish shows a harmonious blend of lighter and darker colors that adds dimension and creates the illusion of greater textural activation.

ALTERNATION – HIGHLIGHTS/ LOWLIGHTS/WEAVING

Draw or fill in the boxes with the appropriate answers.

artist**+**
access.

EXISTING/DESIRED

E   E   E   E   E

D   D   D   D   D

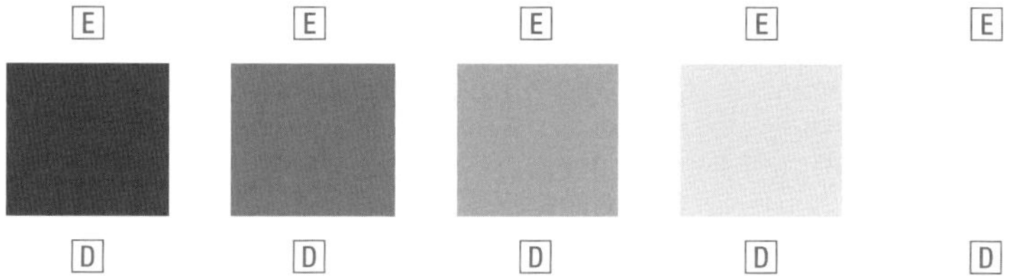

STRUCTURE

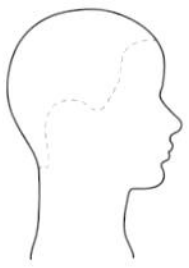

DESIGN PRINCIPLE

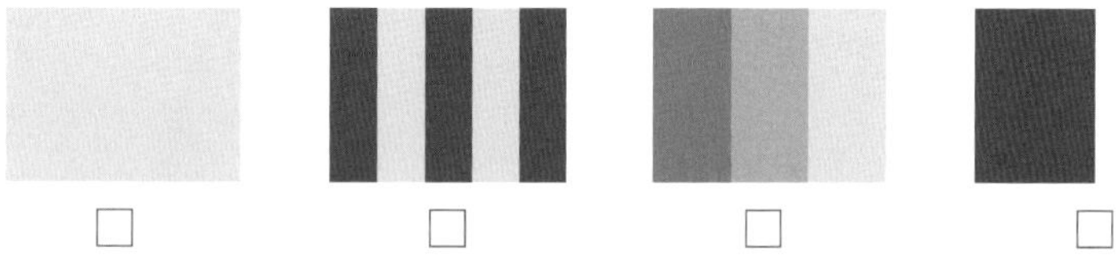

☐   ☐   ☐   ☐

FORM/TEXTURE

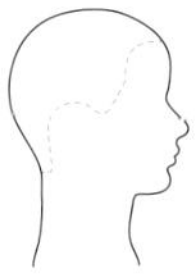

SECTIONING/PARTING PATTERN

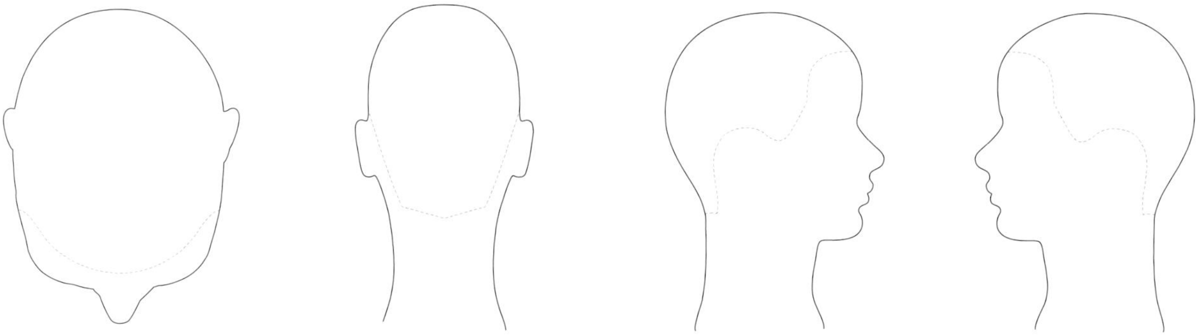

TOOLS/PRODUCT CHOICE

_____
Educator Signature

Date

02

COLOR DESIGN RUBRIC *WORKSHOP 07*

ALTERNATION – HIGHLIGHTS/ LOWLIGHTS/WEAVING

This rubric is a performance assessment tool designed to measure your ability to ***create*** *Pivot Point color designs.*

	LEVEL 1 *in progress*	LEVEL 2 *getting better*	LEVEL 3 *entry-level proficiency*
PREPARATION			
• Assemble color design essentials	☐	☐	☐
CREATE			
• Section head into five sections	☐	☐	☐
• Part diagonally back at hairline in right back section; create medium weaves and apply lightener from edge of foil to ends	☐	☐	☐
• Fold foil upward and then fold once more (double-fold technique)	☐	☐	☐
• Place end of comb under foil and reinforce position close to scalp; fold sides inward	☐	☐	☐
• Use same procedure to apply lowlight color in next foil; colored foil is used to identify lowlights	☐	☐	☐
• Repeat, alternating rows of highlights and lowlights working upward; subdivide wider partings as needed	☐	☐	☐
• Repeat same technique in left back section beginning with highlight foil	☐	☐	☐
• Move to right side, take a diagonal-back parting at hairline, weave and foil beginning with highlight	☐	☐	☐
• Alternate highlights and lowlights using diagonal-back partings and same procedures working to top of section; subdivide wider partings	☐	☐	☐
• Repeat same technique on left side	☐	☐	☐
• Move to top section (center) and take a horizontal parting at front hairline; create medium weave	☐	☐	☐
• Apply highlight to first foil, then apply lowlight color to next foil	☐	☐	☐
• Alternate highlights and lowlights using same procedures working to back of section	☐	☐	☐
• Process color according to manufacturer's instructions	☐	☐	☐
• Remove foils, rinse, shampoo and dry hair	☐	☐	☐
• Apply toner from base to ends on entire head	☐	☐	☐
• Process according to manufacturer's instructions	☐	☐	☐
• Rinse, shampoo, and condition	☐	☐	☐
• Finish color design	☐	☐	☐

TOTAL POINTS = _____ + _____ + _____

TOTAL POINTS _____ ÷ HIGHEST POSSIBLE SCORE 60 X 100 = _____ %

Record your time in comparison with the suggested salon speed.

To improve my performance on this procedure, I need to:

_____   _____   _____
Student Signature   *Educator Signature*   *Date*

WORKSHOP 08
CONTRAST/ ALTERNATION – HIGHLIGHTS/ SLICING

An alternation of color creates the illusion of additional texture in this design. Positioning the highlights within a circular interior zone enhances the appearance of the shape and creates more of a focal point. Deeper perimeter color creates contrast that has a slimming effect on the exterior of the form.

Interior highlights and a darker perimeter create a contrast on this medium field. A violet-based toner is applied over the highlighted area.

The finish shows a contrast of color in which the highlighted area creates a focal point and gives the illusion of added interior texture.

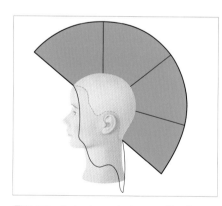

This color design is created on a uniformly layered form.

FORMULA: *Level 4, gold permanent color with 10 volume (3%) developer; lightener with 20 volume (6%) developer.* TONER: *Level 8, violet demi-permanent color with developer.*

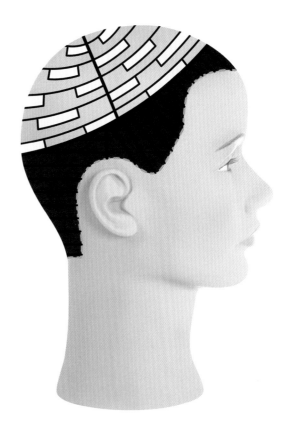

The art shows a circular parting used to section a zone within the interior. The remaining lengths incorporate the entire hairline to create a second zone. The circular zone is sectioned into quadrants and the perimeter zone is sectioned for control. Medium slices in a bricklay pattern will be used in the circular section. Partings will be parallel to the curved sectioning line in the back and front quadrants. Horizontal and diagonal partings will be used to apply color in the perimeter zone.

01 Subsection the circular section into quadrants. Section the perimeter zone for control.

02 Apply barrier cream around the entire hairline.

03 Begin the application by taking a horizontal parting at the nape.

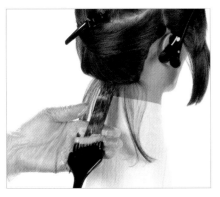

04–05 Apply the deeper color from base to ends starting at the center and working to either side.

06 Release subsequent horizontal partings and repeat the same technique.

07 Maintain consistent partings as you work toward the top of the section, working from the center to either side.

08 As you reach the top of the section, angle the brush near the ear and direct the lengths toward the back to avoid staining the skin.

09 Diagonal-forward partings will be used at the sides. The partings will become less steep as you work around the hairline toward the center front.

10 Take a diagonal-forward parting and apply color from base to ends, carefully directing the hair toward the back.

11 Take consistent diagonal-forward partings as you work toward the front.

12 Adapt the angle of the partings to control lengths as you work to the center front hairline.

13 Repeat the same technique on the other side again using diagonal-forward partings.

14 Adapt the angle of the partings again as you work to the center front hairline.

15 Apply foil to prevent color in the perimeter from touching the hair within the circular zone. If necessary, fold the foil back off of the face.

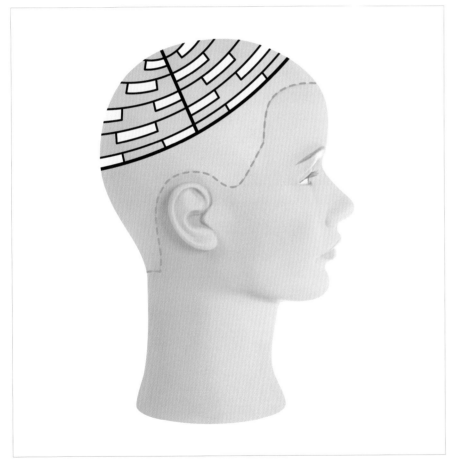

16 The art shows that medium slices, parallel to the sectioning line, will be used within a bricklay pattern in the back and at the sides.

17 Release a ¼" (.6 cm) parting parallel to the perimeter sectioning line and subdivide a slice at one end of the parting. Position a foil underneath the slice.

18 Apply lightener from base to ends, then use a single-fold technique to isolate the section.

19 Bricklay the slices, leaving the center of the parting untreated.

20 Then use the same technique to apply the lightener.

21 Next, release a ½" (1.25 cm) parting. Take a ¼" (.6 cm) slice off the top in the center of the parting to stagger with the previous slices.

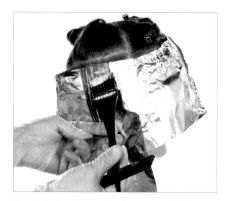

22 Apply lightener using the same technique.

23–24 Work toward the top using ¼" (.6 cm) slices and the bricklay pattern.

25 Move to the other back quadrant and repeat the same techniques, starting at the sectioning line of the shape. Use ¼" (.6 cm) slices and continue the bricklay pattern from the first quadrant.

26 On this side, begin by creating the first slice in the middle of the parting.

27 Work toward the top of the section using a bricklay pattern. Use ½" (1.25 cm) partings and ¼" (.6 cm) slices.

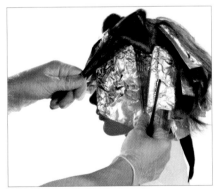

28–30 Move to one of the front quadrants and release a diagonal-back parting at the edge of the shape. Take a ¼" (.6 cm) slice, continuing to stagger with the slices in the previous section. Use the same technique to apply the lightener and fold the foils. Then work to the top of the section using ½" (1.25 cm) partings, ¼" (.6 cm) slices.

31 Repeat the same technique on the other side.

32 The completed application shows foils in a circular interior zone with a darker color applied to the perimeter. Process until the desired degree of lightness is achieved. Rinse thoroughly, then shampoo and dry the hair.

33 Apply the toner to the highlighted area, from base to ends. Process according to the manufacturer's instructions. Then rinse, shampoo, condition and finish as desired.

34–36 The finishes show how the highlights increase the illusion of texture in the design while the deeper perimeter color creates contrast and makes the exterior of the shape appear less rounded.

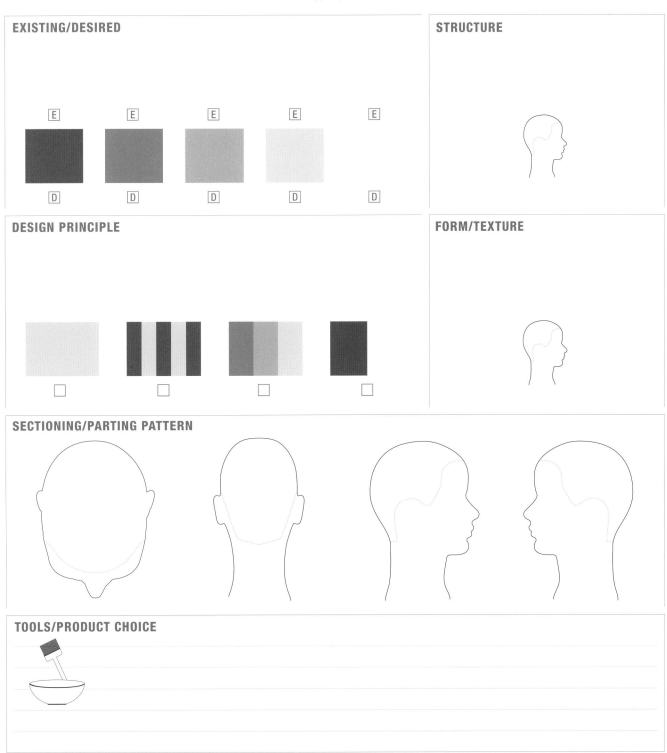

DESIGN DECISIONS *WORKSHOP 08*
CONTRAST/ALTERNATION – HIGHLIGHTS/SLICING artist⁺access.
Draw or fill in the boxes with the appropriate answers.

EXISTING/DESIRED

E E E E E

D D D D D

STRUCTURE

DESIGN PRINCIPLE

FORM/TEXTURE

SECTIONING/PARTING PATTERN

TOOLS/PRODUCT CHOICE

Educator Signature

Date

COLOR DESIGN RUBRIC *WORKSHOP 08*

CONTRAST/ALTERNATION –
HIGHLIGHTS/SLICING

This rubric is a performance assessment tool designed to measure your ability to
create Pivot Point color designs.

	LEVEL 1 *in* *progress*	LEVEL 2 *getting* *better*	LEVEL 3 *entry-level* *proficiency*
PREPARATION			
• Assemble color design essentials	☐	☐	☐
CREATE			
• Section circular zone in interior	☐	☐	☐
• Section remaining perimeter zone below circle for control; section circle into quadrants	☐	☐	☐
• Apply barrier cream around hairline and ears	☐	☐	☐
• Part horizontally across nape using ¼" (.6 cm) parting	☐	☐	☐
• Apply deeper color from base to ends; work from center to either side	☐	☐	☐
• Work up back with ¼" (.6 cm) horizontal partings using the same techniques	☐	☐	☐
• Distribute partings back and angle brush as you work around ear	☐	☐	☐
• Part at sides using ¼" (.6 cm) diagonal-forward partings	☐	☐	☐
• Apply color from base to ends and distribute back	☐	☐	☐
• Adapt angle of partings as you work toward front	☐	☐	☐
• Repeat techniques on opposite side using ¼" (.6 cm) diagonal-forward partings	☐	☐	☐
• Position foil over perimeter lengths	☐	☐	☐
• Release ¼" (.6 cm) parting parallel to sectioning line in one back quadrant of circle	☐	☐	☐
• Subdivide slice at end of parting and place on foil	☐	☐	☐
• Apply lightener from base to ends, enclosing with a single-fold technique	☐	☐	☐
• Bricklay slices in parting, leaving center lengths untreated; use same foil and application techniques	☐	☐	☐
• Release a ½" (1.25 cm) parting parallel to first	☐	☐	☐
• Slice ¼" (.6 cm) off top and in center of parting, creating staggered effect	☐	☐	☐

COLOR DESIGN RUBRIC *WORKSHOP 08* (CONT'D)
CONTRAST/ALTERNATION –
HIGHLIGHTS/SLICING

	LEVEL 1 *in progress*	LEVEL 2 *getting better*	LEVEL 3 *entry-level proficiency*
Apply lightener using same techniques	☐	☐	☐
Work toward top using bricklay pattern and ½" (1.25 cm) partings with ¼" (.6 cm) slices	☐	☐	☐
Position first slice in other back quadrant in center of ¼" (.6 cm) parting parallel to sectioning line	☐	☐	☐
Apply lightener using same techniques	☐	☐	☐
Work toward top using bricklay pattern with ½" (1.25 cm) partings and ¼" (.6 cm) slices	☐	☐	☐
Release ¼" (.6 cm) diagonal-back parting in front quadrant on one side	☐	☐	☐
Apply lightener and fold foils using same techniques, staggering slices	☐	☐	☐
Work toward top of section using ½" (1.25 cm) partings with ¼" (.6 cm) slices	☐	☐	☐
Repeat procedures on other side	☐	☐	☐
Process until desired degree of lightness is achieved	☐	☐	☐
Rinse, shampoo and dry hair	☐	☐	☐
Apply toner in highlighted area from base to ends	☐	☐	☐
Process according to manufacturer's instructions	☐	☐	☐
Rinse, shampoo and condition hair	☐	☐	☐
Finish color design	☐	☐	☐

TOTAL POINTS = _____ + _____ + _____

TOTAL POINTS _____ ÷ HIGHEST POSSIBLE SCORE 102 X 100 = _____ %

Record your time in comparison with the suggested salon speed.

To improve my performance on this procedure, I need to:

_____ _____ _____
Student Signature   Educator Signature   Date

VOICES OF SUCCESS

"Many students are excited and nervous about starting the color design class. I'm glad I can help them build a strong foundation with steps to achieve predictable color design results and give them the tools they need to take their skills into the clinic salon."

THE SALON OWNER

IN OTHER WORDS

With a proven set of coloring procedures and techniques, you will be able to create endless color designs for your clients with precision and skill.

"It's important to me that my clients are informed about how to maintain their color design after they leave the salon. I always show my clients products to take home with them to make sure their color looks just as good during the third week as it did in the first. My number one priority is to make sure my clients always look their best."

THE DESIGNER

"I love that I can trust my designer to listen to my needs and be able to give me the color results I am looking for. At the same time, she's always open with me and gives me advice on what shades she thinks will work best with my skin tone and hair. I'm so happy that I've found someone that I feel comfortable with and can trust with my hair."

THE CLIENT

LEARNING CHALLENGE

Circle the letter corresponding to the correct answer.

1. The standard procedures used to color hair are:
   a. section, part, apply, remove and condition, finish
   b. distribute, scale, part, apply, remove and condition
   c. distribute, scale, process, test, remove and condition
   d. section, part, apply, process, test, remove and condition

2. Which of the following do designers use to identify sectioning in hair coloring?
   a. product
   b. density
   c. facial features
   d. geometric shapes

3. To determine if the color has sufficiently processed, you should:
    a. check the timer
    b. rinse and condition
    c. perform a patch test
    d. perform a strand test

4. Applying a repetition of color to a solid form will:
    a. remove weight
    b. soften the form
    c. enhance the form
    d. enhance activated texture

5. Which of the following is not a common shape used within color design for the graduated form?
    a. circle
    b. square
    c. triangle
    d. rectangle

LESSONS LEARNED

- The six steps that will produce predictable color design results are:
  - Section
  - Part
  - Apply
  - Process
  - Test
  - Remove and Condition
- Color design requires creativity and careful execution using procedural steps to create the final color result.
- Client education about at-home maintenance is essential to maintaining the integrity of the hair.
- Careful considerations should be made to personalize hair color results for each and every client.

ADVANCED COLOR DESIGN

ADAPTING COLOR
TECHNIQUES TO
COMBINATION FORMS
AND USING SPECIALIZED
APPLICATIONS WILL ALLOW
YOU TO OFFER YOUR
CLIENTS PERSONALIZED
COLOR DESIGNS

FOLLOWING THIS LESSON
YOU WILL BE ABLE TO:

List various criteria to consider for advanced color placement when working with combination forms

Describe the importance of communicating with the client about an advanced color design

Demonstrate the knowledge and ability to perform a variety of advanced color designs featuring color placement for specific combination sculpted forms

Demonstrate the knowledge and ability to use specialized color techniques and patterns to create advanced color designs

Successful hair designers can create advanced color designs that make an unmistakable impression—cool, hip and interesting—you can't help but notice. At the same time these designs complement the client beautifully instead of overwhelming him or her. As a designer, you should aspire to help your clients make a color statement that reflects their attributes, personality and sense of style, while keeping their hair in the best possible condition.

In *Chapter 3, Advanced Color Design*, you will get firsthand experience working with advanced color techniques and designs that will expand the possibilities from subtle to outrageous, for you and your clients.

3.1 ADVANCED COLOR DESIGN TECHNIQUES

Now that you have mastered the basics of color design, you are ready to explore the possibilities of more advanced techniques and applications. Combination form color designing and specialized color techniques are used to create this wide range of advanced color results.

COMBINATION FORM COLOR DESIGNING

You already know that color can visually change the appearance of the texture or the form of the design. You can also choose to emphasize a specific area or create a focal point. Since most clients wear combination form sculptures, you will need to constantly adapt your color designs, especially in regard to the color placement on the head or along the strands. For this reason, you need to section based on the following considerations:

- Where longest lengths fall once the hair is finished
- Where in the design the surface texture changes from unactivated to activated
- Where the design is supposed to show volume and expansion
- Where in the design a distinct weight build-up occurs
- In which direction(s) the hair will be worn
- Which styled texture the hair will feature when finished

In other words, sectioning patterns will need to be carefully thought out to be in tune with the combination form sculpture you are working on. Additionally, you'll need to have solid communication skills and use professional language that will allow you to successfully consult with your clients about these color designs.

The advanced color designs featured below will give you an opportunity to study the relationship between color placement and the combination form structures.

A beautiful blend of honey blonds creates textural nuances on the surface with the slightly deeper tones accentuating the solid form line.

A combination of solid and increase-layered forms with a full, heavy fringe is accentuated by back-to-back highlights within an oval-shaped section. To create a harmonious effect and enhance the appearance of the smooth, unactivated interior texture, the lighter tones are carefully positioned at the top of the head to fall within the long, layered lengths.

This leaves the crest and exterior in the deeper tone, accentuating the solid perimeter. The hair is sectioned so that the darker color also is placed along the hairline in the fringe to add strength to the solid line. A "veil" of the deeper tones is left to fall over the highlighted area to further blend the lighter and darker tones.

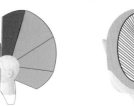

A deeper color adds visual fullness or thickness to the perimeter of this combination form while lighter and brighter tones give the illusion of more volume.

In this combination of graduated, increase-layered and solid forms, an irregular five-point star-shaped section is used to anchor the color placement. One point of the star section is positioned along the side part so the cool, red tone falls on either side of it. Diamond shapes with lighter, warmer tones are positioned between the points of the star. Note how all the points are positioned so that the lengths fall down to reach—but not extend too much into—the more activated area of the design.

In this design, light, medium and dark tones are repeated in a circular pattern in the interior. The dark tone is also applied throughout the perimeter.

The purpose of this color design is to unify the asymmetric form of the sculpture and accentuate the difference between the interior and the tightly stacked, exterior textures. A circle shape is placed near the top of the head so that the darkest color below anchors the entire perimeter and most of the activated texture. Only the longer interior lengths are colored with the lighter and brighter tones.

03

Attention is drawn to the longer interior lengths of this combination form and the texture is greatly enhanced.

Deeper tones throughout the shorter exterior help create the illusion of a close-fitting silhouette. Coloring the base of the interior darker in contrast to lightened and recolorized interior ends creates an effect that makes the texture activation in the interior more apparent. Note that the ends are lightened in an alternating pattern to create the illusion of additional texture activation. Toning the interior lengths with transparent purple shades helps harmonize this contrasting color design.

COLOR CREATIONS

Look at the following illustration and use markers or colored pencils to create a color design. Then use the head sketches to draw the structure graphic you believe matches the form shown. Draw your color pattern on the other head sketch and explain your choices of color placement using the blank lines provided.

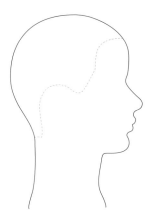

SPECIALIZED TECHNIQUES AND PATTERNS

Another way to create advanced color designs can be to apply color with specialized techniques and patterns. These techniques require that you "think outside the box" and push your coloring skills to new levels of creativity. These techniques may require new and unusual tools or a different type of application with a standard tool. They may be more freeform in nature, relying heavily on your artistic vision and ability to control your application.

COLOR SCRUNCHING

Not all specialized application techniques are complex. Here, lightener is scrunched onto the ends of curly, layered hair to create dimensional color that accentuates the curled texture. It is important to observe the curl patterns carefully and to apply consistently to the ends of the hair. As with many freehand techniques, a delicate touch is required.

DOUBLE-PROCESS BLOND

At first glance, this may not seem like an advanced technique, but a virgin application of lightener requires a very accurate and efficient application. It also requires the designer to monitor decolorization and recolorization carefully. Executing a double-process blond color design that maintains the integrity of the hair requires great skill.

COLOR MELTING

Placing color along the strand according to your design plan requires that you visualize the results and accurately apply each color along the strand proportionately.

GUIDELINES FOR ADVANCED COLOR DESIGNING

It is certainly part of human nature to grow tired of what we are familiar with and want a change. As a designer you will encounter many clients who are ready for somethng new. This is where many designers find creative opportunities to offer change to their clients. Color changes can range from very subtle and discreet to a dramatic transformation. Color design offers the option of changing back or trying something different yet again, not long after the initial visit. So, it's easy to build a loyal clientele who are excited to return for the next visit.

COMMUNICATION GUIDELINES

The following chart will help you respond to the most common client cues in a way that encourages a client to try an advanced color design service, while building client trust and loyalty.

CLIENT CUE	DESIGNER RESPONSE
"Can you believe how cold the weather got all of the sudden? It really feels like fall now."	*"I agree. I always marvel at how beautiful fall colors are. Have you already switched your wardrobe over and maybe bought some new pieces? I could see a few interesting color designs for you that would beautifully finish off your new style for fall. You know, as your summer tan slowly fades, we can work with some rich hair colors to give you a fresh look."*
"I am really starting to get tired of my gray hair! My biggest concern about coloring is that it might look unnatural."	*"Oh, I can help you out with that. Natural hair colors look natural because they are actually a blend of many different shades. Natural hair colors are also always just a hint lighter around the face and darker in the nape. Since our skin pigmentation gets more fair as we gray, I would use a color about one level lighter than your natural color and add fine, subtle highlights and lowlights to blend harmoniously. This way, your gray will be gone and the color you'll have will perfectly complement your complexion and look rich and natural."*
"Wow, I really love that new haircut you just gave me. I feel like a different person!"	*"I am so glad you like it. It looks really great on you. Now that your hair has a much more distinct shape, I think we should look at a zonal color pattern to bring out your beautiful bone structure and accentuate the haircut even more. Let me show you some ideas."*
"I would love for my curly hair to be a bit lighter and softer, but I've had highlights before and they just didn't work with my curls."	*"That can happen when standard highlights are done on hair with a curl like yours. What I recommend is that we just gently lighten the ends of your hair by scrunching color onto them. Then we could follow with a color rinse to add additional shine and warmth. This way your color will be lighter and brighter while taking advantage of your curls. By the way, this color requires little upkeep and will blend well on days you choose to wear your hair straight."*

3.2 ADVANCED COLOR DESIGNS

At this point in your color design training, you are ready to go out and practice some of the advanced color techniques that appeal to your creative side as well as to a wider range of color clients. These designs will build on what you already know about color and the basic techniques you have practiced.

ADVANCED WORKSHOP 01
ALTERNATION – PARTIAL HIGHLIGHTS/ SLICING

This color design is ideal for clients who desire a versatile color design that can appear more subdued or intense depending on styling. Slices and a back-to-back foiling technique are used to create a subtle blend of colors that can be styled to be more or less obvious.

Note that different-colored foils are used to identify the color formulas.

A back-to-back slicing technique is used to introduce two colors within the interior and fringe lengths on this medium-light field.

The finish shows an exposure of two soft blond colors, which enhances both the activated and unactivated textures of this elongated shape.

This color design is created on a combination of solid and increase-layered forms with a full face-framing fringe.

FORMULA: *Lightener with 20 volume (6%) developer; level 8, beige permanent color with 20 volume (6%) developer; level 7, gold demi-permanent color with developer.*

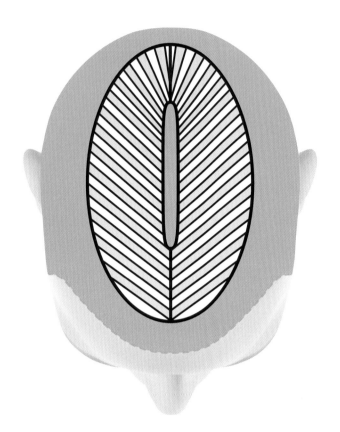

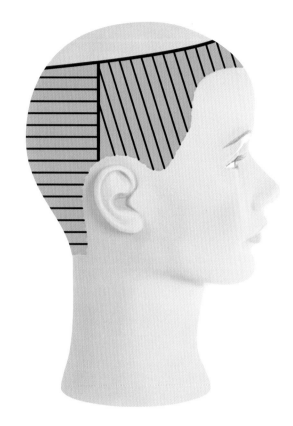

The art shows that an oval-shaped section is used in the interior. A narrow section at the center top parallels the center part and extends slightly into the fringe. The hair in this section will act as a veil that falls over the colored sections. Back-to-back diagonal-back slices will be used on either side of this section. Horizontal and diagonal-forward partings will be used in the back and sides to apply color to the remaining lengths.

01 Section the head as shown above.

02–03 Begin at the front on one side. Take a fine diagonal-back slice at the front of the shape. Position a foil beneath the slice and apply lightener from the base to the ends. Fold the foil using a single-fold technique.

04 Now release another slice directly above the first one. Apply level 8, beige from base to ends.

05–06 Continue working toward the back, alternating between the lightener and beige. Use the back-to-back slicing technique, leaving no hair between the slices.

07 Adapt the diagonal slices as you work toward the back of the shape and over the curves of the head.

08 The last slice at the center back is almost vertical and finer than the previous ones. Apply lightener.

09 Now, move to the opposite side and begin at the front of the shape. Again, use a fine diagonal-back slice and apply lightener to this first slice from base to ends.

10–11 Release the next slice and apply the level 8, beige. Repeat the sequence as you work toward the back using back-to-back diagonal slices and alternating the colors.

12 To complete this side, a very fine slice with lightener will be positioned next to the fine slice on the opposite side. Note that these two slices combined equal the width of the previous slices used.

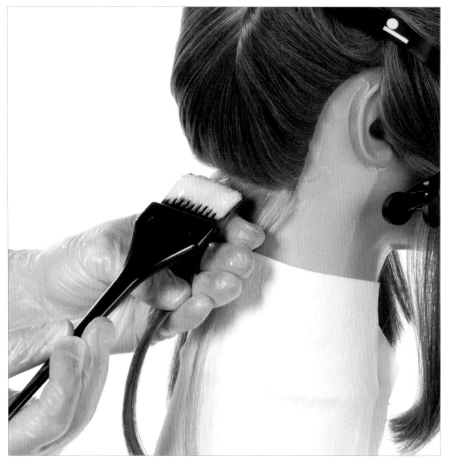

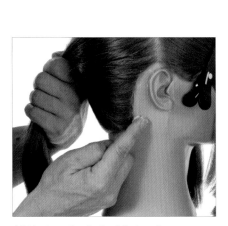

13 Next, gently clip the foiled sections up and out of the way and section the exterior at the ears. Then apply barrier cream around the hairline.

14 Move to the nape and take a ¼" (.6 cm) horizontal parting. Apply a level 7, gold demi-permanent color from base to ends, starting at the center.

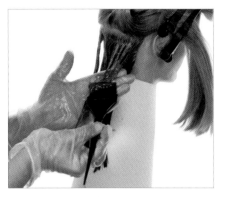

15–16 Work from the center to either side. Work toward the top of the back section.

17 Angle your brush to direct the hair back as you work toward the side.

18 On the sides, ¼" (.6 cm) diagonal-forward partings are used.

19 Apply color from base to ends, directing the lengths back and away from the face.

20 Work toward the front hairline. Gently lay each parting back and away from the face as you work. Be sure to apply color carefully at the front hairline to avoid staining the skin. Repeat on the opposite side.

21–22 Unclip the foils and release the narrow section at the center top. Split the section in half and apply the level 7, gold color from base to ends to one half, then to the other half.

23 Process according to the manufacturer's instructions. Rinse the gold color first, then rinse the beige color and finally the lightener. Shampoo, condition and finish as desired.

24–25 The finish shows a beautiful blend of soft blond colors, made more evident by the slightly darker tones underneath and the veil on the top surface.

DESIGN DECISIONS *ADVANCED WORKSHOP 01*
ALTERNATION – PARTIAL HIGHLIGHTS/SLICING artist⁺access.

Draw or fill in the boxes with the appropriate answers.

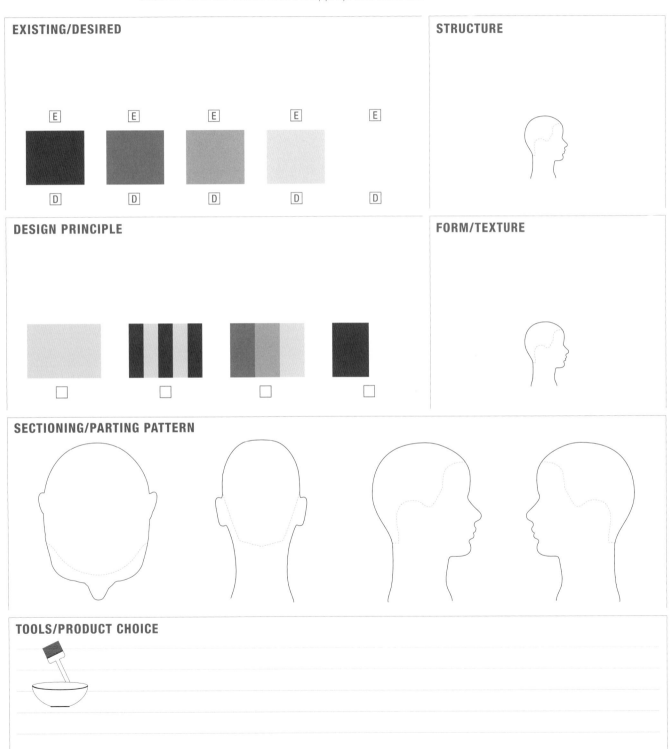

EXISTING/DESIRED

STRUCTURE

DESIGN PRINCIPLE

FORM/TEXTURE

SECTIONING/PARTING PATTERN

TOOLS/PRODUCT CHOICE

Educator Signature

Date

COLOR DESIGN RUBRIC *ADVANCED WORKSHOP 01*

ALTERNATION – PARTIAL HIGHLIGHTS/SLICING

This rubric is a performance assessment tool designed to measure your ability to ***create*** *Pivot Point color designs.*

	LEVEL 1 *in progress*	LEVEL 2 *getting better*	LEVEL 3 *entry-level proficiency*
PREPARATION			
• Assemble color design essentials	☐	☐	☐
CREATE			
• Section an oval-shaped section in interior and a narrow section at center top extending the length of center part and slightly into fringe	☐	☐	☐
• Take a fine diagonal-back slice at front of shape on one side	☐	☐	☐
• Position foil beneath slice; apply lightener from base to ends	☐	☐	☐
• Fold foil using single-fold technique	☐	☐	☐
• Release another slice, directly above first slice; apply beige color using same technique	☐	☐	☐
• Continue working toward back, alternating between lightener and beige, using back-to-back slicing technique	☐	☐	☐
• Adapt diagonal slices while working toward back of shape	☐	☐	☐
• Part last slice almost vertically and finer than previous slices; apply lightener from base to ends	☐	☐	☐
• Move to opposite side; begin at front of shape and take a fine diagonal-back slice; apply lightener using same technique	☐	☐	☐
• Release another slice; apply beige using same technique	☐	☐	☐
• Continue alternating between lightener and beige working toward back of shape	☐	☐	☐
• Position a very fine slice next to fine slice on opposite side; apply lightener from base to ends	☐	☐	☐

COLOR DESIGN RUBRIC *ADVANCED WORKSHOP 01* (CONT'D)
ALTERNATION – PARTIAL HIGHLIGHTS/SLICING

	LEVEL 1 *in progress*	LEVEL 2 *getting better*	LEVEL 3 *entry-level proficiency*
Clip foiled sections up and out of way gently; section exterior at ears	☐	☐	☐
Apply barrier cream around hairline	☐	☐	☐
Move to nape; take a ¼" (.6 cm) horizontal parting	☐	☐	☐
Apply level 7, gold demi-permanent color from base to ends starting at center	☐	☐	☐
Work from center to either side using same technique	☐	☐	☐
Work toward top of back section	☐	☐	☐
Angle brush to direct hair back while working toward side	☐	☐	☐
Take ¼" (.6 cm) diagonal-forward partings on sides	☐	☐	☐
Apply color from base to ends, directing lengths back and away from the face	☐	☐	☐
Work toward front hairline using same technique, laying each parting gently back and away from the face	☐	☐	☐
Apply color carefully at front hairline to avoid staining skin	☐	☐	☐
Repeat same technique on opposite side	☐	☐	☐
Unclip foils and release narrow section at center top; split section in half	☐	☐	☐
Apply level 7, gold color from base to ends to one half, then the other	☐	☐	☐
Process according to manufacturer's instructions	☐	☐	☐
Rinse, shampoo and condition	☐	☐	☐
Finish as desired	☐	☐	☐

TOTAL POINTS = _____ + _____ + _____

TOTAL POINTS _____ ÷ HIGHEST POSSIBLE SCORE 90 X 100 = _____ %

Record your time in comparison with the suggested salon speed.

To improve my performance on this procedure, I need to:

Student Signature   Educator Signature   Date

ADVANCED WORKSHOP 02
CONTRAST – ZONES

Deeper tones are used in the perimeter of this design. Lighter and brighter tones used in diamond-shaped sections and in a star-shaped zone create a fashion-forward finish on this combination form.

Dark brown, medium red and light copper colors are used in zones to create harmonious contrast in this color design. The existing color is a medium-light field.

The darkest color is used around the entire perimeter, which contrasts with the light color above it. The medium color at the top allows the light color to peek through.

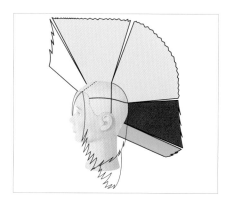

This color design is created on a sculpture that combines graduated, increase-layered and solid forms.

FORMULA: *Medium level 6, red permanent color with 20 volume (6%) developer; level 7, copper gold permanent color with 30 volume (9%) developer; dark level 5, brown permanent color with 10 volume (3%) developer.*

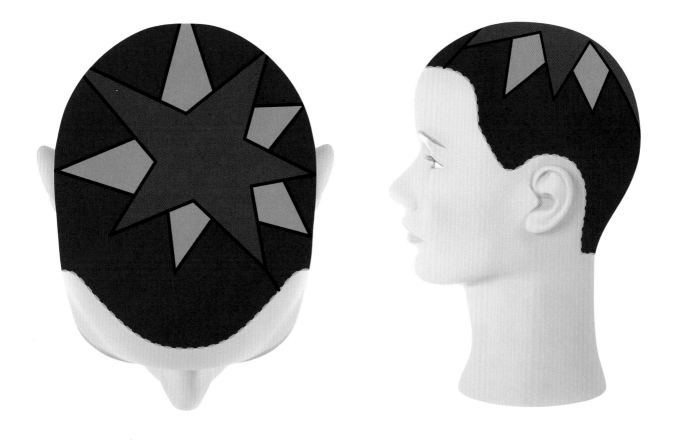

The art shows an off-center, irregular five-point star-shaped section, with one point at the side part. Between the points, diamond-shaped sections will be used. Note that the irregular shape of the star may cause some of the diamond shapes to be irregular as well.

01–02 Section an irregular, off-center star on top of the head, starting with a point at the side part. Then section diamond shapes between the points of the star. Section the perimeter zone for control.

03 Apply barrier cream to the skin along the hairline to prevent stains.

04 Release a ¼" (.6 cm) horizontal parting in the nape. Apply the darkest color from base to ends beginning in the center and working to either side.

05 Continue to work up the back. Above the ears, direct the strands back as the color is applied to avoid staining the skin.

06 When you reach the areas between the points of the upper shapes, carefully apply the dark color between the points, working in one area at a time.

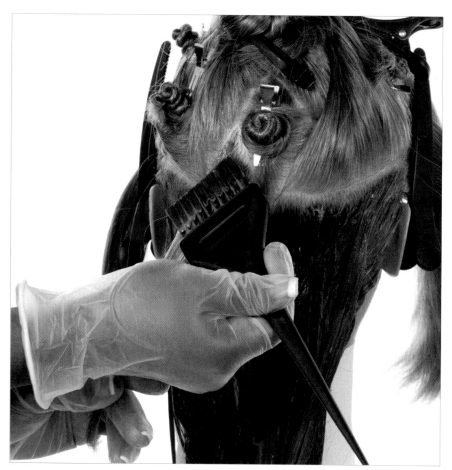

07 Work to the top of each area using ¼" (.6 cm) horizontal partings. Angle the brush as necessary to avoid having color come into contact with the other sections.

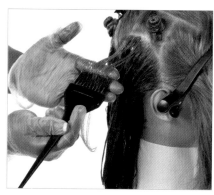

08 Work through the remainder of the back.

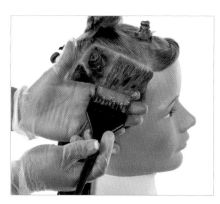

09 Move to one side and release a ¼" (.6 cm) diagonal-forward parting. Apply the dark color from base to ends. Then direct the hair toward the back to prevent product from staining the skin.

10 Adapt the angle of the partings as you work through the perimeter zone. Work up to the side part. Use the same techniques to complete the other side.

11 Check the hairline to ensure even coverage and apply more product if needed.

12–13 Position thermal strips over the completed zone. Line up the edges of the strips to the edges of the upper shapes. Note that the strips may be folded back at the face. Release the diamond shapes.

14 Begin in the front diamond shape. Take a ¼" (.6 cm) parting at the outer tip of the shape and position a thermal strip under the parting. Apply the lightest color from base to ends.

15 Work through the shape using ¼" (.6 cm) partings. Angle your brush to distribute the product in small areas with more precision. Note that only one thermal strip is used under each diamond shape.

16 Place a thermal strip over the completed section. Line up the edge of the thermal strip with the edge of the shape. Note that the ends do not need to be covered.

17 Work through the following sections and apply the lightest color using the same techniques.

18 Work around the head to complete the diamond-shaped sections.

19 The art shows the subsections and partings used in the irregular, off-center star shape at the top. Part from the top of each diamond to the center of the star to create diamond-shaped subsections and secure.

20 Beginning in the front, position a thermal strip under the first ¼" (.6 cm) parting and apply the medium color from base to ends. Work through the shape.

21 Repeat the same procedures through the remaining diamond-shaped subsections of the star.

22 Process according to manufacturer's instructions. Rinse, shampoo, condition and style as desired.

23–25 The finish shows a medium, vibrant red color with a lighter copper color peeking through that contrasts with the dark brown around the perimeter. The effect is a color design that is fashion-forward without being too strong.

CONTRAST – ZONES
Draw or fill in the boxes with the appropriate answers.

EXISTING/DESIRED

E   E   E   E   E

D   D   D   D   D

STRUCTURE

DESIGN PRINCIPLE

☐   ☐   ☐   ☐

FORM/TEXTURE

SECTIONING/PARTING PATTERN

TOOLS/PRODUCT CHOICE

Educator Signature

Date

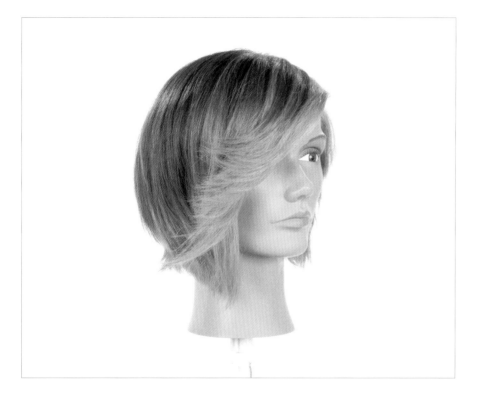

VARIATION 01
CONTRAST – ZONES

The same sectioning based on a star shape used in the previous design will also be used here. In this variation, the perimeter remains lighter and the deeper tone is positioned at the top. An alternation of colors in the diamond shapes further enhances the transition of the color contrast.

Darker and lighter blond tones are used to create this color design on a combination of increase-layered and graduated lengths. The same star- and diamond-shaped sectioning as in the previous exercise is used. The level 9, beige blond is applied in the perimeter zone from base to ends. Then, thermal strips are positioned over the completed zone. Next, an alternation of the red blond and light blond colors is applied from base to ends within each diamond-shaped section, starting at the outside point and using medium-thick slices. The lengths are enclosed in foils. This technique is used in each diamond, starting at the front. The darkest blond color is then applied to the star-shaped section. The color is processed according to manufacturer's instructions, rinsed, shampooed, conditioned and finished.

FORMULA: *Level 10, light blond with 40 volume (12%) developer; level 8, red with 10 volume (3%); level 9, beige blond with 20 volume (6%); level 6, dark blond with 10 volume (3%) developer.*

CONTRAST – ZONES

This rubric is a performance assessment tool designed to measure your ability to **create** *Pivot Point color designs.*

	LEVEL 1 *in progress*	LEVEL 2 *getting better*	LEVEL 3 *entry-level proficiency*
PREPARATION			
• Assemble color design essentials	☐	☐	☐
CREATE			
• Section an irregular, off-center star shape on top of the head	☐	☐	☐
• Section diamond shapes between the star's points; section perimeter zone for control	☐	☐	☐
• Apply barrier cream to skin along hairline	☐	☐	☐
• Release a ¼" (.6 cm) horizontal parting at nape	☐	☐	☐
• Apply dark color from base to ends, working from center to either side	☐	☐	☐
• Repeat procedures, working up back	☐	☐	☐
• Direct strands back as color is applied above ears	☐	☐	☐
• Apply dark color in areas between upper shapes one at a time using same procedures	☐	☐	☐
• Angle brush as needed; complete back	☐	☐	☐
• Release a ¼" (.6 cm) diagonal-forward parting on one side	☐	☐	☐
• Apply dark color from base to ends; direct lengths back	☐	☐	☐
• Adapt angle of partings around the front perimeter zone and work up to side part	☐	☐	☐
• Repeat procedures on opposite side	☐	☐	☐
• Apply product to hairline as needed	☐	☐	☐
• Position thermal strips over completed zone; line up edge of strip with upper shapes	☐	☐	☐
• Release diamond-shaped sections; begin in front	☐	☐	☐
• Release ¼" (.6 cm) parting at outer tip of shape; position thermal strip under parting	☐	☐	☐
• Apply light color from base to ends, working through section; angle brush as necessary	☐	☐	☐
• Complete section using same techniques; position thermal strip over section	☐	☐	☐
• Repeat techniques working around head and completing diamond-shaped sections	☐	☐	☐
• Release star shape; subsection star into diamond shapes and secure	☐	☐	☐
• Begin in front; position thermal strip under a ¼" (.6 cm) parting	☐	☐	☐
• Apply medium color from base to ends	☐	☐	☐
• Repeat techniques working up section	☐	☐	☐
• Apply medium color through each diamond-shaped subsection of star using same procedures	☐	☐	☐
• Process according to manufacturer's instructions	☐	☐	☐
• Rinse, shampoo and condition	☐	☐	☐
• Finish color design as desired	☐	☐	☐

TOTAL POINTS = _____ + _____ + _____

TOTAL POINTS _____ ÷ HIGHEST POSSIBLE SCORE 87 X 100 = _____ %

Record your time in comparison with the suggested salon speed. _____

To improve my performance on this procedure, I need to: _____

_____   _____   _____
Student Signature   Educator Signature   Date

ADVANCED WORKSHOP 03

REPETITION – VIRGIN LIGHTER

A virgin-lighter technique is used in this exercise to achieve the lightest range of hair colors. During a double process, the hair is decolorized, or lightened, to a desired degree. Then a toner is applied to neutralize unwanted tones.

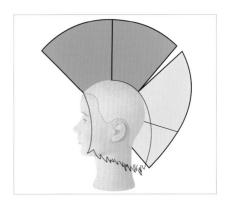

A light blond is achieved by prelightening this medium field to palest yellow, then toning it to achieve a light neutral blond. This is often referred to as a double-process color design.

A repetition of color is achieved on this combination of uniformly layered and graduated lengths.

FORMULA: *On-the-scalp lightener with 20 volume (6%) developer.* TONER: *Level 10, violet demi-permanent color with developer.*

The art shows that the head will be sectioned in quadrants for control. One-eighth inch (.3 cm) horizontal partings will be used to apply lightener in the back and slight diagonal-back partings will be used in the front.

01 Section the head into four sections from the center front hairline to the center back and from the top of the head to each ear.

02 Apply barrier cream around the hairline and to the tops of the ears to protect the skin.

03–04 Begin in the back right section by releasing a ⅛" (.3 cm) horizontal parting in the nape, which is usually the darkest area. Apply lightener from approximately ½" (1.25 cm) away from the scalp through the ends, thoroughly saturating the strands. Then place cotton at the base to prevent seepage.

05 Work toward the top. Subdivide wider partings and use two pieces of cotton as needed.

06 Maintain consistent ⅛" (.3 cm) horizontal partings, applying lightener generously to each strand to complete the section.

07–08 Repeat on the opposite side. Start at the nape and work toward the top to complete the entire back section.

10 Work toward the top. Subdivide wider partings for control.

09 Move to the front. On one side, take a ⅛" (.3 cm) slightly diagonal-back parting at the bottom and apply lightener ½" (1.25 cm) away from the base through the ends, being sure to thoroughly saturate the strand.

11 Work to the center sectioning line using consistent ⅛" (.3 cm) slight diagonal-back partings.

12 Repeat on the opposite side to complete the front sections.

13 At this point, cotton should still be placed securely at the base of each parting.

14 Strand test for the desired degree of decolorization. Remove the lightener with a damp towel to clearly see the results.

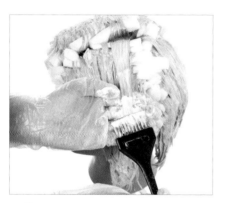

15 Reapply the lightener as necessary.

16–17 When the hair has decolorized halfway to the desired degree of lightness, remove the cotton beneath the first parting at the top of the back right section. Apply lightener to the top and bottom of the strand at the base. Continue removing the cotton from subsequent partings and applying lightener. Apply generously to ensure even application.

18 Work toward the bottom of the section, applying lightener to the top and bottom of each strand at the base to complete the section.

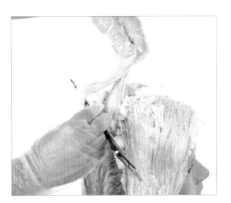

19–20 Next, carefully bring each parting down. Apply lightener to the base of each parting on the other side. Then carefully bring these lengths down.

21 Move to the front and work from the top to the bottom to complete both sections. Note that as an option, all cotton may be removed prior to the application of lightener at the base.

22 Cross-check the application using vertical partings to ensure complete coverage. Then re-apply lightener to the entire hairline.

23 Once the desired degree of decolorization is achieved, rinse, shampoo and dry the hair. Be sure that the desired degree of lightness is achieved before applying the toner. Note that the decolorization should be uniform from base to ends.

REPETITION – VIRGIN LIGHTER

Draw or fill in the boxes with the appropriate answers.

artist**+**
access.

EXISTING/DESIRED

E   E   E   E   E

D   D   D   D   D

STRUCTURE

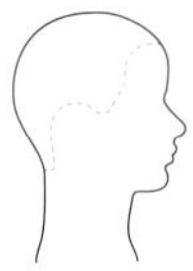

DESIGN PRINCIPLE

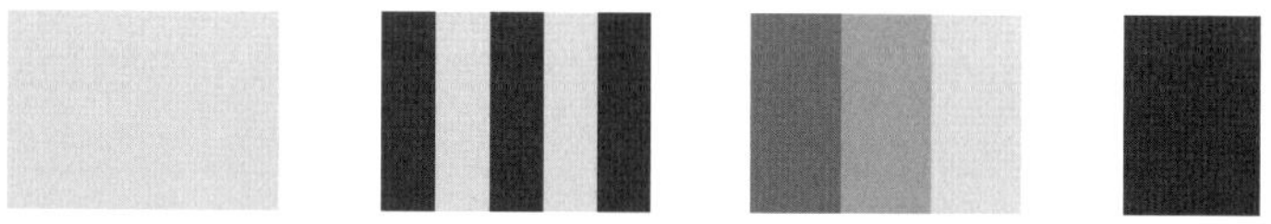

FORM/TEXTURE

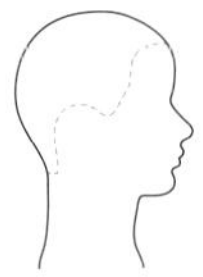

SECTIONING/PARTING PATTERN

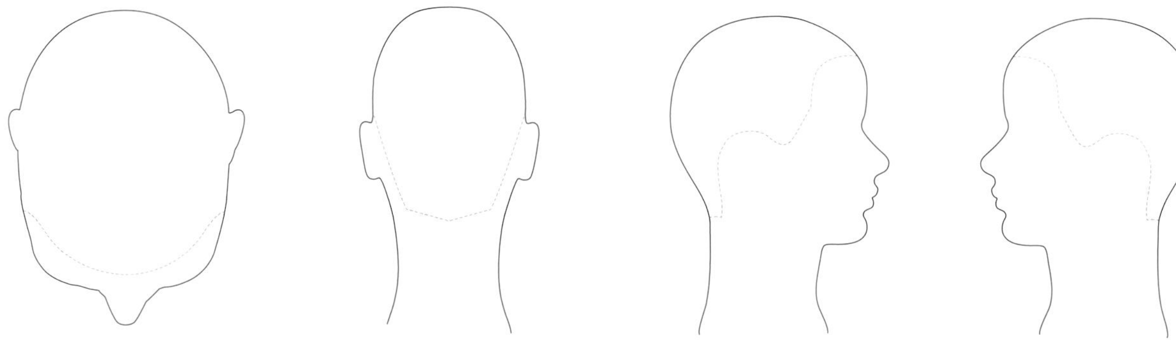

TOOLS/PRODUCT CHOICE

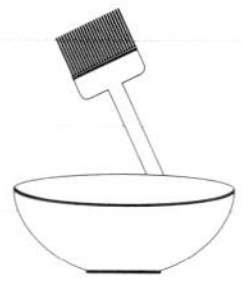

18 Work toward the bottom of the section, applying lightener to the top and bottom of each strand at the base to complete the section.

19–20 Next, carefully bring each parting down. Apply lightener to the base of each parting on the other side. Then carefully bring these lengths down.

21 Move to the front and work from the top to the bottom to complete both sections. Note that as an option, all cotton may be removed prior to the application of lightener at the base.

22 Cross-check the application using vertical partings to ensure complete coverage. Then re-apply lightener to the entire hairline.

23 Once the desired degree of decolorization is achieved, rinse, shampoo and dry the hair. Be sure that the desired degree of lightness is achieved before applying the toner. Note that the decolorization should be uniform from base to ends.

25 Use the tip of the applicator bottle to release a ¼" (.6 cm) horizontal parting at the top of one of the back sections.

26 Apply the toner from base to ends to the top and bottom of the strand. Work the color into the strand using your thumb and the tip of the applicator bottle.

24 The art shows that ¼" (.6 cm) horizontal partings will be used to apply the toner in the back and ¼" (.6 cm) diagonal-back partings will be used in the front.

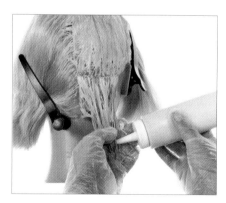

27-28 Work toward the bottom of the section, subdividing wider areas for control.

29 After completing the section, bring the lengths down. Repeat on the other side to complete the entire back section.

30 Move to the front and use ¼" (.6 cm) diagonal-back partings and the same application technique, starting at the top of each section. Generously saturate each strand while applying.

31 Use the tip of the bottle to work the toner through the lengths and direct the hair away from the face.

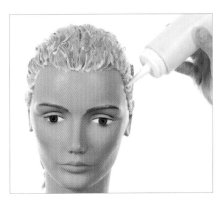

32 Next, apply toner around the entire hairline to ensure even coverage.

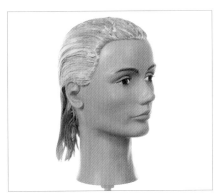

33 Process according to the manufacturer's instructions. Then rinse, shampoo, condition and finish as desired.

34-35 The finish shows a beautiful, light neutral blond with even and consistent color throughout. Careful application and processing help keep the hair in optimum condition.

REPETITION – VIRGIN LIGHTER
Draw or fill in the boxes with the appropriate answers.

EXISTING/DESIRED

E E E E E

D D D D D

STRUCTURE

DESIGN PRINCIPLE

☐ ☐ ☐ ☐

FORM/TEXTURE

SECTIONING/PARTING PATTERN

TOOLS/PRODUCT CHOICE

Educator Signature

Date

VARIATION 02
REPETITION – VIRGIN LIGHTER

In this variation, the virgin-lighter technique is performed using a single process, high-lift color. A single process can only be performed using a permanent color, which has the ability to lift and deposit color. Because of its unusual porosity, when performing a virgin-lighter technique on chemically processed hair, using color instead of lightener is gentler and safer.

A high-lift color with a copper base is used to create a repetition of color on this graduated form with a solid fringe. The head is sectioned in quadrants and barrier cream is applied around the entire hairline. Starting at the nape, color is applied to ¼" (.6 cm) horizontal partings from ½" (1.25 cm) away from the scalp through to the ends. Cotton is placed at the base to prevent product seepage. The same technique is used to complete the back sections. Slightly diagonal-back partings are used on both of the front sections, starting at the bottom, working toward the top. When the hair reaches approximately 50% development, freshly mixed color is applied to the base after removing the cotton, starting at the top of the first back section and working toward the nape. After completing the back sections, the same technique is used to complete both front sections. Then, color is re-applied to the entire hairline and the application is cross-checked to ensure complete coverage. The color is processed according to manufacturer's instructions, then rinsed, shampooed, conditioned and finished as desired.

FORMULA: *High-lift color with level 8, copper permanent color with 30 volume (9%) developer.*

COLOR RUBRIC *ADVANCED WORKSHOP 03*
REPETITION – VIRGIN LIGHTER
This rubric is a performance assessment tool designed to measure your ability to **create** *Pivot Point color designs.*

	LEVEL 1 *in progress*	LEVEL 2 *getting better*	LEVEL 3 *entry-level proficiency*
PREPARATION			
• Assemble color design essentials	☐	☐	☐
CREATE			
• Section using four sections; center front hairline to center back; from ear to ear	☐	☐	☐
• Apply barrier cream around the hairline and tops of ears	☐	☐	☐
• Release ⅛" (.3 cm) horizontal parting in nape in right back section	☐	☐	☐
• Apply lightener approximately ½" (1.25 cm) away from scalp through ends; place cotton at base	☐	☐	☐
• Work toward top using same technique	☐	☐	☐
• Subdivide wider partings; use two pieces of cotton as needed	☐	☐	☐
• Repeat same application technique on opposite side starting at nape	☐	☐	☐
• Move to front on one side; take ⅛" (.3 cm) slightly diagonal-back parting at bottom; apply lightener using same technique	☐	☐	☐
• Work toward top; subdivide wider partings for control	☐	☐	☐
• Work to center sectioning line using consistent ⅛" (.3 cm) slight diagonal-back partings	☐	☐	☐
• Repeat same technique on opposite side	☐	☐	☐
• Strand test for desired degree of decolorization; remove lightener with a damp towel	☐	☐	☐
• Reapply lightener as necessary	☐	☐	☐
• Remove cotton beneath first parting at top of back right section when hair has decolorized halfway to the desired degree of lightness	☐	☐	☐
• Apply lightener at the base, to top and bottom of strand	☐	☐	☐
• Work toward bottom of section using same technique	☐	☐	☐

COLOR RUBRIC *ADVANCED WORKSHOP 03* (CONT'D)
REPETITION – VIRGIN LIGHTER

	LEVEL 1 in progress	LEVEL 2 getting better	LEVEL 3 entry-level proficiency
Bring each parting down	☐	☐	☐
Repeat same technique on other side	☐	☐	☐
Move to front; complete both sides using the same technique; work from top to bottom	☐	☐	☐
Cross-check application using vertical partings	☐	☐	☐
Re-apply lightener to the entire hairline	☐	☐	☐
Rinse, shampoo and dry hair, once desired degree of decolorization is achieved	☐	☐	☐
Release ¼" (.6 cm) horizontal parting at top of one of back sections using tip of applicator bottle	☐	☐	☐
Apply toner from base to ends to top and bottom of strand	☐	☐	☐
Work color into strand using thumb and tip of applicator bottle	☐	☐	☐
Work toward bottom of section using same technique	☐	☐	☐
Subdivide wider areas for control	☐	☐	☐
Bring lengths down	☐	☐	☐
Repeat same technique on other side	☐	☐	☐
Move to front; use ¼" (.6 cm) diagonal-back partings and same application technique, starting at top of each section	☐	☐	☐
Work toner through lengths using tip of bottle; direct hair away from face	☐	☐	☐
Apply toner around entire hairline	☐	☐	☐
Process according to manufacturer's instructions	☐	☐	☐
Rinse, shampoo and condition	☐	☐	☐
Finish as desired	☐	☐	☐

TOTAL POINTS = _____ + _____ + _____

TOTAL POINTS _____ ÷ HIGHEST POSSIBLE SCORE 108 X 100 = _____ %

Record your time in comparison with the suggested salon speed.

To improve my performance on this procedure, I need to:

Student Signature   Educator Signature   Date

ADVANCED WORKSHOP 04
ALTERNATION – HIGHLIGHTS/ SLICING

To avoid results that are too obvious, or to adapt a pattern that reflects a specific styling direction, a slightly irregular or freeform sectioning pattern may be used. Only designers who are skilled and confident in their technical application should venture into this type of design approach.

A slicing technique is used to introduce an alternation of two colors throughout the interior and front of this dark field. The back exterior is left natural.

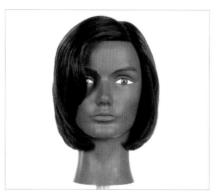

The finish shows a harmonious blend of warm tones, which adds textural interest.

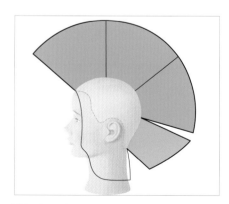

This alternation of two colors is created on a uniformly layered form with a solid perimeter.

FORMULA: *High-lift gold color with 30 volume (9%) developer; high lift red copper color with 30 volume (9%) developer.*

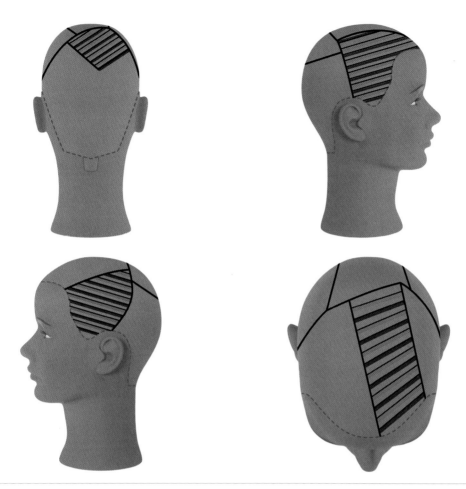

The art shows the head is sectioned with a rectangle positioned diagonally from the crown to the front hairline on the left. The sides are sectioned with diagonal lines from the back corners of the rectangle to the front of each ear. Diagonal lines are used behind the rectangle to section an irregular diamond or kite-shaped section. Medium-fine slices are used to alternate colors within each section.

01 Section the head as shown above.

02–03 Begin at the shape in the back. Take a medium-fine slice adjacent to the diagonal line on the right side. Position a foil beneath the slice and apply the red copper color from base to ends. Fold the foil using a single-fold technique.

04 Next, release a diagonal-left parting and take a medium-fine slice from the top of the parting. Use the same technique to apply the gold color. Note that the color of the foil helps to identify the color.

05–06 Work toward the top of the section. Use consistent diagonal-left partings and alternate between the red copper and gold colors. Note that the slices at the top of the shape are shorter to accommodate the irregular shape.

08 Apply the red copper color from base to ends, then use a single-fold technique to fold the foil.

09 Apply the gold color to the next slice.

07 Move to the right side and release a diagonal-back parting at the bottom of the section. Take a medium-fine slice from the top.

10 Work toward the top of the section, alternating between the red copper and gold formulas. As partings become too wide, subdivide for control and use two or more foils as needed.

11 Apply color from base to ends within each foil.

12 If necessary, tilt the head for ease of application as you reach the top.

13 Move to the opposite side and use diagonal-back slices. Alternate the two colors as you work toward the top.

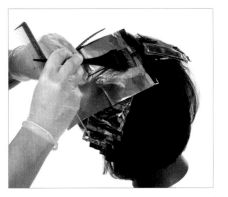

14–15 This section will be narrower at the top. After applying the color, fold the foil upward. Then fold each side toward the center and continue to fold multiple times to create a narrower foil packet.

16 Next, move to the rectangular section at the top. Release a thin parting at the hairline, and take a medium-fine slice off the top of it.

17–18 Apply the red copper color from base to ends and fold the foil. Work toward the back of the section using parallel medium-fine slices. Alternate colors and tilt the head forward if necessary. Note that the last parting is almost parallel to the back of the rectangular shape.

19 The completed application shows the alternation of foils used to indicate the alternation of color formulas. Process according to the manufacturer's directions. Rinse, shampoo, condition and finish as desired.

20-21 The finish shows a beautiful blend of warm colors that brightens the overall look, while harmonizing with the natural color at the back of the design.

DESIGN DECISIONS *ADVANCED WORKSHOP 04*
ALTERNATION – HIGHLIGHTS/SLICING
Draw or fill in the boxes with the appropriate answers.

EXISTING/DESIRED

E   E   E   E   E

D   D   D   D   D

STRUCTURE

DESIGN PRINCIPLE

☐   ☐   ☐   ☐

FORM/TEXTURE

SECTIONING/PARTING PATTERN

TOOLS/PRODUCT CHOICE

Educator Signature   *Date*

COLOR RUBRIC *ADVANCED WORKSHOP 04*
ALTERNATION – HIGHLIGHTS/SLICING
This rubric is a performance assessment tool designed to measure your ability to
***create** Pivot Point color designs.*

	LEVEL 1 *in progress*	LEVEL 2 *getting better*	LEVEL 3 *entry-level proficiency*
PREPARATION			
• Assemble color design essentials	☐	☐	☐
CREATE			
• Section a rectangle positioned diagonally from the crown to the front hairline on the left; section sides with diagonal lines from back corners of rectangle to front of each ear; section an irregular diamond- or kite-shaped section behind rectangle	☐	☐	☐
• Take a medium-fine slice adjacent to diagonal line on right side of shape in back	☐	☐	☐
• Position foil beneath slice; apply red copper color from base to ends	☐	☐	☐
• Fold foil using single-fold technique	☐	☐	☐
• Release a diagonal-left parting; take a medium-fine slice from top of parting	☐	☐	☐
• Apply gold color from base to ends	☐	☐	☐
• Work toward top of section using same technique, alternating between red copper and gold colors to complete section	☐	☐	☐
• Move to right side; release a diagonal-back parting at bottom of section	☐	☐	☐
• Take a medium-fine slice trom top	☐	☐	☐
• Apply red copper color from base to ends	☐	☐	☐
• Fold foil using single-fold technique	☐	☐	☐
• Repeat same technique to apply gold color	☐	☐	☐
• Work toward top of section, alternating between red copper and gold formulas	☐	☐	☐
• Subdivide for control using two or more foils for wider areas to complete section	☐	☐	☐
• Move to opposite side; use diagonal-back slices and same foiling technique	☐	☐	☐
• Alternate between the two colors while working toward the top	☐	☐	☐
• Apply color to narrow top area; fold foil upward, then fold each side toward center; fold multiple times to create a narrower foil packet to complete section	☐	☐	☐
• Move to rectangular section at top; release thin parting at hairline; take a medium-fine slice off top	☐	☐	☐
• Work toward back of section using parallel medium-fine slices to alternate colors	☐	☐	☐
• Process according to manufacturer's directions	☐	☐	☐
• Rinse, shampoo and condition	☐	☐	☐
• Finish color design as desired	☐	☐	☐

TOTAL POINTS = _____ + _____ + _____

TOTAL POINTS _____ ÷ HIGHEST POSSIBLE SCORE 69 X 100 = _____ %

Record your time in comparison with the suggested salon speed.

To improve my performance on this procedure, I need to:

_____   _____   _____
Student Signature   *Educator Signature*   *Date*

ADVANCED WORKSHOP 05
CONTRAST – HIGHLIGHTS/ SCRUNCHING

Creating a color design that enhances or visually alters the form and/or texture of a client's hair design is one of the joys of being a designer. One way in which curlier textures can be enhanced is by using a technique called "scrunching" This technique involves applying lightener or color onto the surface of the hair using a motion not unlike that used to scrunch when air forming.

Lightener is gently scrunched onto the ends of this medium field. Then a copper blond, nonoxidative semi-permanent color is applied to the entire head.

The finished design shows textural definition with enhanced depth and dimension.

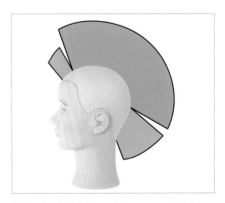

This color design is created on a combination form that features uniform layers and a solid perimeter accented by a shorter fringe.

FORMULA: *Powder lightener with 20 volume (6%) developer.* TONER: *Level 8, copper blond semi-permanent color.*

01 Air form the hair with a scrunching technique to exaggerate the curl patterns. Do not apply styling products.

02 Begin by applying an even amount of lightener onto the entire inner portion of the gloved hand. Note that lightener should be a consistency that won't drip or clump.

03 Begin the application at the center back perimeter, and gently scrunch lightener onto the surface. Avoid working lightener too far into the hair.

04–05 Work from the center to either side. Continue to apply the same amount of product to your glove and work for consistent application of product throughout the area.

06 Work upward in a consistent manner. Using the scrunching technique to apply lightener onto the surface.

07–08 Work from the center to either side. Gently squeeze and release each section without pulling.

09 Continue to use the same technique as you apply lightener working toward the top.

10 Make sure that the product is applied evenly to both sides.

11 Apply lightener to the remaining top lengths, leaving the front perimeter natural.

12 Here we see the completed application of lightener. Process to the desired level of lightness. Rinse, shampoo, then air form the hair.

 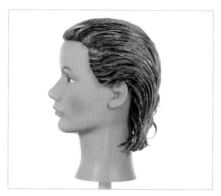

13–14 Next, apply a copper blond, nonoxidative color using a bottle application. Apply to the entire head from base to ends. Process according to manufacturer's instructions. Rinse, shampoo, condition and style as desired.

15–16 Adding light reflections on ends of curly textured hair adds interest and complements the shape while accentuating the texture. Bright, intense colors or soft, natural tones can be used to create a diffused color effect such as this.

DESIGN DECISIONS *ADVANCED WORKSHOP 05*
CONTRAST – HIGHLIGHTS/SCRUNCHING
Draw or fill in the boxes with the appropriate answers.

artist**+**
access.

EXISTING/DESIRED

E   E   E   E   E

D   D   D   D   D

STRUCTURE

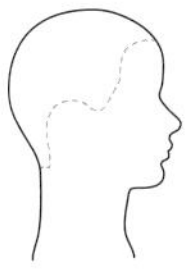

DESIGN PRINCIPLE

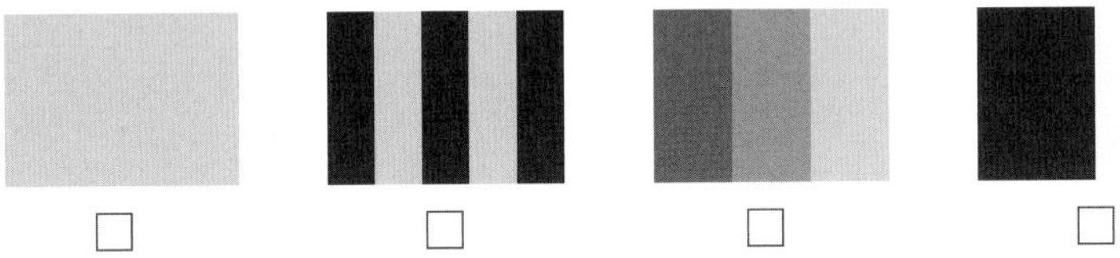

☐   ☐   ☐   ☐

FORM/TEXTURE

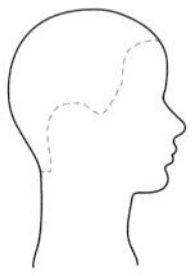

SECTIONING/PARTING PATTERN

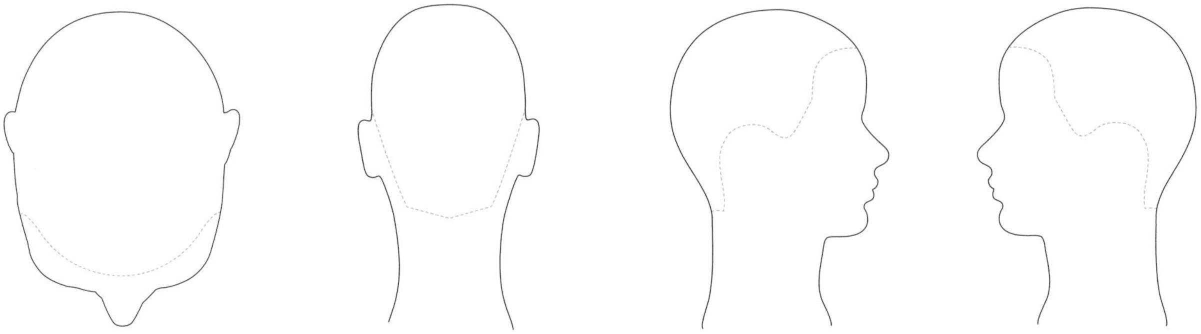

TOOLS/PRODUCT CHOICE

Educator Signature

Date

COLOR RUBRIC *ADVANCED WORKSHOP 05*
CONTRAST – HIGHLIGHTS/SCRUNCHING
This rubric is a performance assessment tool designed to measure your ability to **create** *Pivot Point color designs.*

	LEVEL 1 *in progress*	LEVEL 2 *getting better*	LEVEL 3 *entry-level proficiency*
PREPARATION			
• Assemble color design essentials	☐	☐	☐
CREATE			
• Air form hair using scrunching technique; do not apply styling products	☐	☐	☐
• Apply consistent, even amount of lightener onto entire inner portion of hand	☐	☐	☐
• Scrunch lightener gently onto surface starting at center back perimeter; avoid working lightener too far into hair	☐	☐	☐
• Work from center to either side; continue to apply same amount of product to glove; work for consistent application of product throughout area	☐	☐	☐
• Work upward in a consistent manner; continue using scrunching technique to apply lightener onto surface	☐	☐	☐
• Work from center to either side	☐	☐	☐
• Gently squeeze and release each section without pulling; avoid applying lightener to lengths that may touch skin around hairline	☐	☐	☐
• Apply lightener working toward top using same technique	☐	☐	☐
• Repeat same technique on opposite side; make sure product is applied evenly to both sides	☐	☐	☐
• Apply lightener to remaining top lengths, leaving front perimeter natural	☐	☐	☐
• Process to desired level of lightness	☐	☐	☐
• Rinse, shampoo and air form hair	☐	☐	☐
• Apply a copper blond, nonoxidative color using a bottle application	☐	☐	☐
• Apply to entire head from base to ends	☐	☐	☐
• Process according to manufacturer's instructions	☐	☐	☐
• Rinse, shampoo and condition	☐	☐	☐
• Finish as desired	☐	☐	☐

TOTAL POINTS = _____ + _____ + _____

TOTAL POINTS _____ ÷ HIGHEST POSSIBLE SCORE 54 X 100 = _____ %

Record your time in comparison with the suggested salon speed.

To improve my performance on this procedure, I need to:

_____   _____   _____

Student Signature   *Educator Signature*   *Date*

ADVANCED WORKSHOP 06
ALTERNATION – ZONES/CIRCLE

In this design, an alternation of dark, medium and light colors in a circular interior zone effectively contrasts the repetition of the dark color in the exterior. The use of triangular sections from a point of origin creates a beautiful blend of colors that falls and moves over the curve of the head. The design can be worn to make a bolder, more obvious color statement or for a softer look that reflects the appearance of colors in nature.

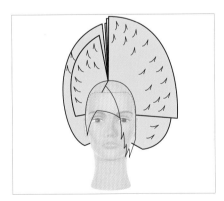

Three colors are used to add tonality and depth to this medium-light field. The light, medium and dark tones are repeated in a circular pattern within the interior. The dark tone is also applied throughout the perimeter.

This circle color design is created on an asymmetric graduated form.

FORMULA: *Level 4, brown permanent color with 10 volume (3%) developer; level 6, red permanent color with 20 volume (6%) developer; level 7, copper permanent color with 30 volume (9%) developer.*

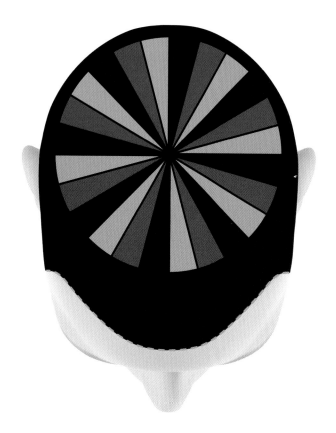
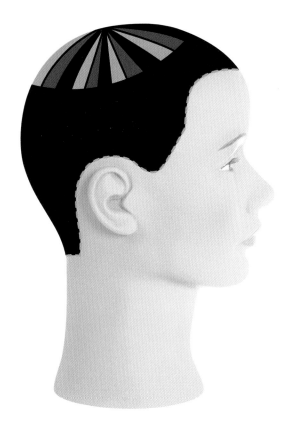

The art shows that pivotal partings will be taken from a point of origin within the circle. Three colors will be applied within this section. Horizontal and vertical partings will be used to apply the darkest color to the exterior.

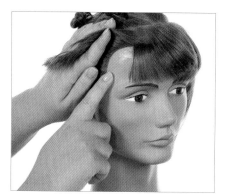

01 Create a circular section that incorporates the top and crown. Divide the circle into four sections. The intersection of these dividing lines will serve as the point of origin.

02–03 Apply barrier cream around the entire hairline. Begin application of the darkest color in the nape. Apply from base to ends using horizontal partings.

04 At the side, apply the color using vertical partings.

05 Work to the front ensuring that color is applied thoroughly around the hairline. Repeat on the opposite side.

06 Next, take a thin triangular or pivotal parting from the point of origin in the back right interior section. Position a foil beneath the part and apply the darkest color from base to ends.

07 Place a different color foil over the color. Note that different colored foils are used to identify the color formulas.

08 Take another triangular section and apply the lightest color from base to ends. Cover the hair with a different-colored foil.

09 Apply the medium color to the third section. Be sure to align the corner of each foil with the point of origin as you progress around it.

10 Repeat the color sequence as you continue the application, working clockwise around the head.

11 Continue to pivot around the head form as you apply color to each section.

12 When you reach the last section of the circle, temporarily fold the foil from the first section out of your way. Continue using the same color sequence to the last pivotal parting.

13 The finished application shows the radial placement of the foils. Process according to manufacturer's instructions, then remove the foils. Rinse, shampoo, condition and finish as desired.

14–15 Colors radiating from a point of origin can create a diffusion of colors, which varies depending on how the hair is designed.

DESIGN DECISIONS *ADVANCED WORKSHOP 06*
ALTERNATION – ZONES/CIRCLE
Draw or fill in the boxes with the appropriate answers.

artist**+**
access.

EXISTING/DESIRED

E E E E E

D D D D D

STRUCTURE

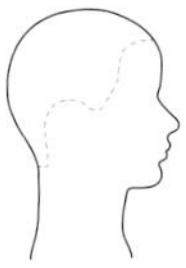

DESIGN PRINCIPLE

☐ ☐ ☐ ☐

FORM/TEXTURE

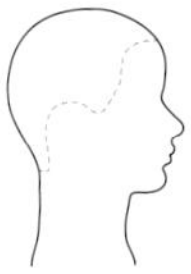

SECTIONING/PARTING PATTERN

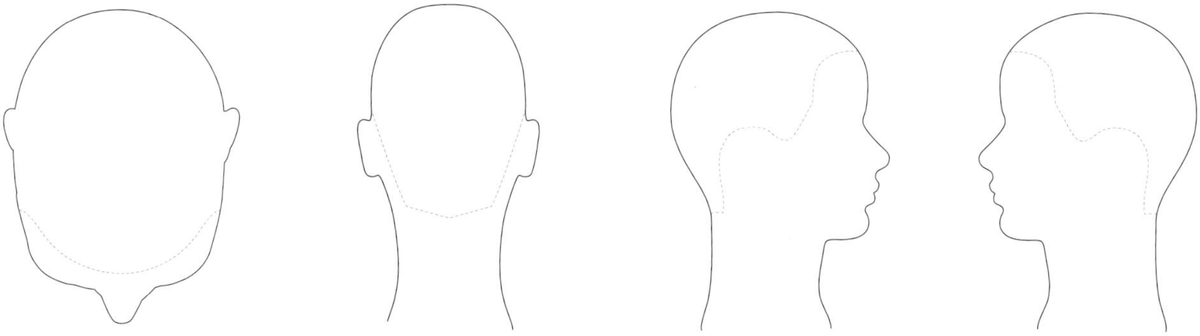

TOOLS/PRODUCT CHOICE

Educator Signature

Date

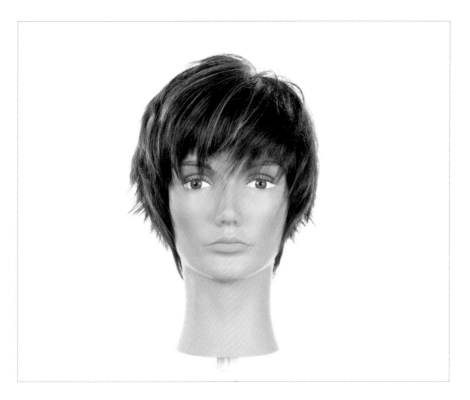

VARIATION 03
ALTERNATION – ZONES/CIRCLE

As in the previous design, a circular section is the basis for this variation. An alternation of color and lightener is positioned within the circle and the remaining hair is deepened to create a richer overall color scheme.

An alternation of colors within a circular interior zone contrasts with the deeper exterior and perimeter to complement this combination form. After sectioning the circle in the interior, it is diagonally sectioned in half. Barrier cream is applied around the hairline. Starting at the left side of the back section, a medium diagonal slice is taken, and a level 7, red color is applied from base to ends and enclosed in foil. A section of hair is left natural, then the same technique is used to apply lightener to the next diagonal slice. The sequence is repeated across the back half of the circle, adapting the angle of the slices as you reach the opposite side. The same technique and color sequence are used in the front half of the circle, starting on the right side, altering the position of the slices. The exterior, perimeter and hair left between the foiled slices are colored using a level 6, natural, applying the color from base to ends. The color is processed according to manufacturer's instructions, then rinsed, shampooed, conditioned and finished.

FORMULA: *Lightener with 20 volume (6%) developer; level 7, red permanent color with 10 volume (3%) developer; level 6, natural permanent color with 10 volume (3%) developer.*

COLOR RUBRIC *ADVANCED WORKSHOP 06*
ALTERNATION – ZONES/CIRCLE

This rubric is a performance assessment tool designed to measure your ability to **create** *Pivot Point color designs.*

	LEVEL 1 *in progress*	LEVEL 2 *getting better*	LEVEL 3 *entry-level proficiency*
PREPARATION			
• Assemble color design essentials	☐	☐	☐
CREATE			
• Section hair into interior circle divided in four sections and exterior zone	☐	☐	☐
• Apply barrier cream around hairline	☐	☐	☐
• Apply darkest color in nape from base to ends using horizontal partings	☐	☐	☐
• Part vertically through sides and work to front hairline	☐	☐	☐
• Repeat on opposite side	☐	☐	☐
• Take a triangular or pivotal parting in back right interior section	☐	☐	☐
• Place foil beneath the part and apply darkest color from base to ends	☐	☐	☐
• Cover section with foil	☐	☐	☐
• Take another triangular or pivotal parting and apply light color from base to ends	☐	☐	☐
• Cover with different color foil	☐	☐	☐
• Take another triangular or pivotal parting and apply medium color from base to ends	☐	☐	☐
• Cover with different color foil	☐	☐	☐
• Continue same technique, alternating color and foil while working clockwise through interior circle	☐	☐	☐
• Process according to manufacturer's instructions	☐	☐	☐
• Rinse, shampoo and condition hair	☐	☐	☐
• Finish as desired	☐	☐	☐

TOTAL POINTS = _____ + _____ + _____

TOTAL POINTS _____ ÷ HIGHEST POSSIBLE SCORE 51 X 100 = _____ %

Record your time in comparison with the suggested salon speed. _____

To improve my performance on this procedure, I need to: _____

_____   _____   _____
Student Signature   *Educator Signature*   *Date*

CONTRAST – BASE AND ENDS

A base-and-ends technique is ideal for clients who desire a striking dimensional color design. The contrast in color can range from bold to subtle, depending on the colors chosen, sculpted texture and desired effect.

A contrast of color was created on this medium-light field. Longer interior lengths were prelighted, then recolorized with a violet color. The base and remaining lengths were darkened.

The finish shows a contrast of color in which interior lengths are accentuated.

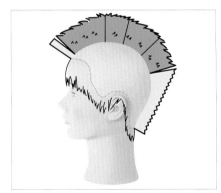

A contrast of color is designed to complement this combination of graduated and uniformly layered lengths.

FORMULA: *Lightener with 20 volume (6%) developer; level 4, natural brown with 10 volume (3%) developer. TONER: Level 7, violet semi-permanent color.*

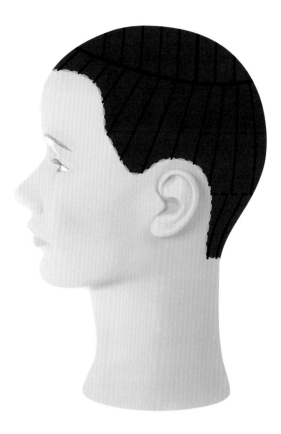

The art shows an oval-shaped section in the interior, which is subdivided to control shorter lengths. Color will be applied to the remainder of the hair using vertical partings at the back and slightly diagonal partings at the sides and the front. Horizontal partings will be used to apply color only to the base within the oval-shaped interior section. Note that these partings are only approximate when working with the very short lengths at the nape.

01 Create an oval-shaped section in the interior and subdivide the oval into three sections.

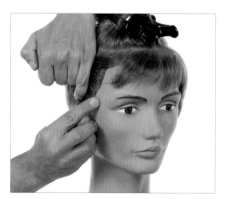

02 Apply barrier cream around the entire hairline to prevent staining.

03 Begin at the center nape. Use the brush to separate the lengths vertically and apply color from base to ends.

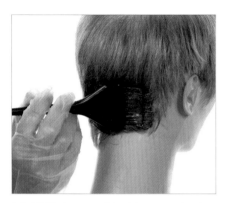  

04–05 Work to one side of the nape using the same technique. You may also use the other hand to help control the lengths. Then work from the center to the other side of the nape. Use the tail of the color brush to lift the hair away from the scalp.

06 In the upper back, use thin vertical partings and apply color using the same technique. Work from the center toward one ear.

07 Then work from the center to the other side to complete the back.

08–09 Move to one side and use slightly diagonal partings to apply the color. Adapt the partings as you work toward the front. Position the brush parallel to the front hairline and direct the lengths away from the face. Work to the center front then repeat on the opposite side.

10 The art shows that horizontal partings will be used to apply color only at the base within the oval-shaped interior section.

11–12 Release the back section and release a horizontal parting at the front of the section. Apply color to the top and bottom of the strand only at the base. Work from the center to one side, then the other side. Continue toward the back. Apply color consistently to the base only.

13 Apply color generously to ensure that the bases blend with the exterior lengths that have been previously colored from base to ends.

14–15 Next, release a front section. Starting at the back of the section, use horizontal partings and apply color to both sides of the strand, only at the base. Work to the front.

16 Use the end of the brush to lift the base so the ends remain in an upright position.

17–18 Repeat the same technique on the other front section. Begin at the back of the section and work to the front.

20 Starting at the back section, take a pivotal parting on one side. Without disturbing the color at the base, split the parting in half and apply lightener to the ends of the outer portion.

19 The art shows that pivotal partings will be used in the back portion of the interior section and horizontal partings will be used within the front half, which is sectioned with a center part. Lightener will be applied to the ends of approximately half of each parting in an alternating pattern.

21 Take another pivotal parting and apply the lightener to the ends of the inner portion. Work to the other side, alternating between the inner and outer portions of each parting.

22–23 Begin at the back of the front section with a horizontal parting on one side of the center part. Split the parting in half and apply lightener to the ends of the inner portion. Work toward the front of the section, alternately applying lightener to the inner or outer strand. Repeat on the other side, staggering the lightened strands with those on the first side.

24 Process until the desired degree of lightness is achieved. Rinse, shampoo and towel-blot the hair thoroughly.

25 Apply a semi-permanent violet color over the entire interior section. Process according to manufacturer's instructions. Rinse, shampoo, condition and finish as desired.

26-27 The finish shows a striking contrast of color that enhances the activated texture within the interior.

CONTRAST – BASE AND ENDS
Draw or fill in the boxes with the appropriate answers.

artist⁺access

EXISTING/DESIRED

E   E   E   E   E

D   D   D   D   D

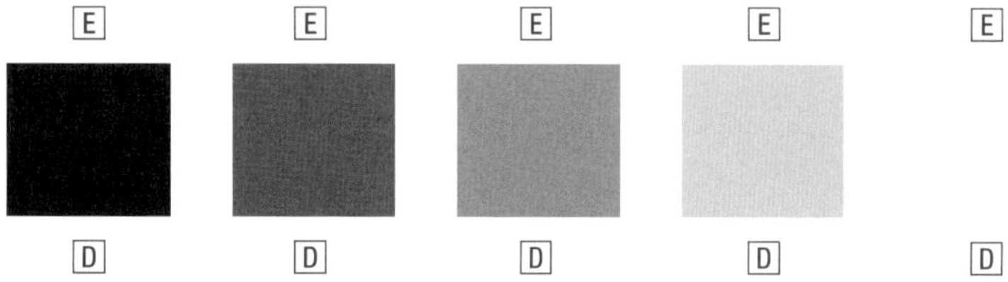

STRUCTURE

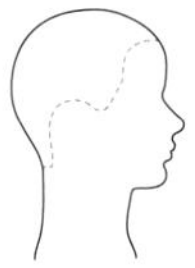

DESIGN PRINCIPLE

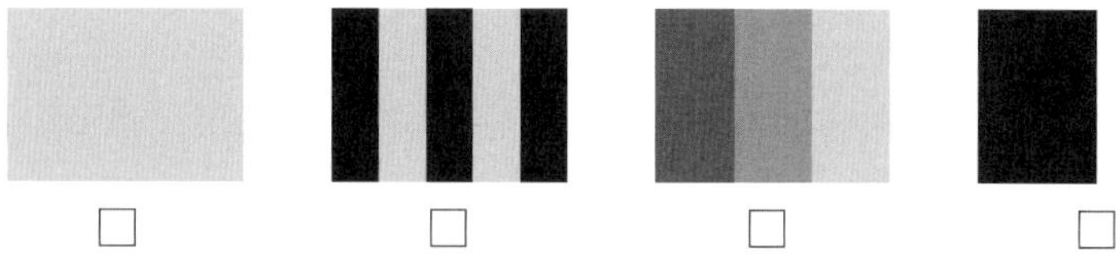

☐   ☐   ☐   ☐

FORM/TEXTURE

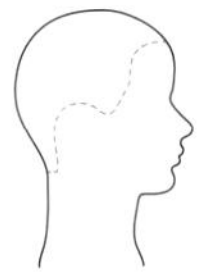

SECTIONING/PARTING PATTERN

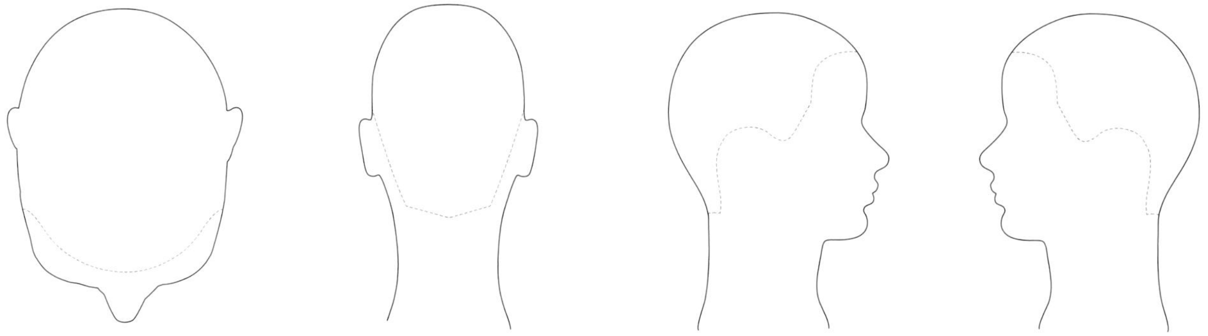

TOOLS/PRODUCT CHOICE

Educator Signature

Date

03

COLOR RUBRIC *ADVANCED WORKSHOP 07*
CONTRAST – BASE AND ENDS
This rubric is a performance assessment tool designed to measure your ability to ***create*** *Pivot Point color designs.*

	LEVEL 1 *in progress*	LEVEL 2 *getting better*	LEVEL 3 *entry-level proficiency*
PREPARATION			
• Assemble color design essentials	☐	☐	☐
CREATE			
• Section an oval-shaped section in interior; subdivide into three sections	☐	☐	☐
• Apply barrier cream around entire hairline	☐	☐	☐
• Begin at center nape; separate lengths vertically using brush and apply color from base to ends to both sides of strand	☐	☐	☐
• Work to one side of nape using same technique; use other hand to help control lengths	☐	☐	☐
• Work from center to other side of nape	☐	☐	☐
• Apply color using thin vertical partings at upper back; work from center toward one ear	☐	☐	☐
• Work from center to other side using same technique to complete back section	☐	☐	☐
• Move to one side; apply color using slightly diagonal partings and same technique	☐	☐	☐
• Adapt partings while working toward front	☐	☐	☐
• Position brush parallel to front hairline; direct lengths away from face	☐	☐	☐
• Work to center front	☐	☐	☐
• Repeat same technique on opposite side	☐	☐	☐
• Release back interior section and release a horizontal parting at front of section	☐	☐	☐
• Apply color to top and bottom of strand, only at base	☐	☐	☐
• Work from center to one side, then to other side	☐	☐	☐
• Continue using same technique while working toward back	☐	☐	☐
• Apply to ensure that bases blend with lengths that have been previously colored from base to ends	☐	☐	☐

CONTRAST – BASE AND ENDS

	LEVEL 1 *in progress*	LEVEL 2 *getting better*	LEVEL 3 *entry-level proficiency*
Release a front section; start at back of section and apply color to both sides of strand, only at base; use horizontal partings	☐	☐	☐
Work toward front using same technique	☐	☐	☐
Lift base so ends remain in an upright position using end of application brush	☐	☐	☐
Repeat same technique on other front section	☐	☐	☐
Take a pivotal parting at one side of back section without disturbing color at base	☐	☐	☐
Split parting in half and apply lightener to ends of outer portion	☐	☐	☐
Take another pivotal parting using same technique; apply lightener to ends of inner portion	☐	☐	☐
Work to other side alternating between inner and outer portions of each parting	☐	☐	☐
Begin at back of front section with a horizontal parting on one side of center part	☐	☐	☐
Split parting in half and apply lightener to ends of inner portion	☐	☐	☐
Work toward the front of section using same technique, applying lightener alternately to inner or outer strand	☐	☐	☐
Repeat same technique on other side, staggering lightened strands with those on first side	☐	☐	☐
Process until desired degree of lightening is achieved	☐	☐	☐
Rinse, shampoo and towel-blot hair thoroughly	☐	☐	☐
Apply semi-permanent violet color over entire interior section	☐	☐	☐
Process according to manufacturer's instructions	☐	☐	☐
Rinse, shampoo and condition	☐	☐	☐
Finish as desired	☐	☐	☐

TOTAL POINTS = _____ + _____ + _____

TOTAL POINTS _____ ÷ HIGHEST POSSIBLE SCORE 108 X 100 = _____ %

Record your time in comparison with the suggested salon speed.

To improve my performance on this procedure, I need to:

_____   _____   _____
Student Signature   *Educator Signature*   *Date*

VOICES OF SUCCESS

"I've been able to build a great reputation for myself with my color designs. I always try to be unique and keep up with the latest trends. Then I use my technical ability and imagination to adapt the trends for my clients!"

THE DESIGNER

"I tend to get bored wearing the same look for a long time. Lucky for me, my colorist is more than able to keep up with me! She creates beautiful color designs. Sometimes, we just change things up a bit; other times, we go for the drama! And she never compromises the health and integrity of my hair. She lets me know what the limits are and I love the results!"

THE CLIENT

"With all the baby boomers on our client roster, we make it a top priority to have first-rate colorists on our staff. We stress the importance of continuing education and carefully crafted color designs. I think it shows in our results—so many loyal clients!"

THE SALON OWNER

IN OTHER WORDS

Taking an advanced approach to color design incorporates well-calculated color placement adapted to combination forms, as well as advanced techniques and patterns, to give hair designers a more competitive edge with a range of creative options.

LEARNING CHALLENGE

Circle the letter corresponding to the correct answer.

1. When designing color for a combination form, which of the following is NOT a consideration designers follow?
    a. how often the client shampoos her hair
    b. where a distinct weight build-up occurs
    c. in which direction(s) the hair will be worn
    d. where longest lengths fall once the hair is finished

2. Coloring the base of a short, layered interior darker in contrast to lighter ends creates the illusion of:
    a. less volume
    b. more length
    c. smoother texture
    d. increased texture activation

3. Applying deeper colors at the perimeter will:
    a. make the hair fuller
    b. add width to the form
    c. reduce visual weight in the perimeter
    d. add visual fullness or thickness to the perimeter

4. Which of the following is NOT a requirement for a successful freehand coloring technique?
    a. a delicate touch
    b. a color design plan
    c. artistic vision and ability
    d. a difficult application procedure

5. A double-process virgin lightener application requires the designer to closely monitor decolorization and:
    a. highlighting
    b. recolorization
    c. the hair length
    d. freehand coloring

LESSONS LEARNED

- Many clients want to explore advanced color designs to create a look that helps them express their personal sense of style.

- When designing for combination forms, it is important to adapt the color placement to the structure of the hair sculpture.

- Advanced color designs require a step-by-step process that incorporates advanced techniques and patterns as well as adaptations of basic techniques and patterns.

- A virgin-lighter technique using lightener is considered an advanced technique because of the amount of skill and accuracy that must be used to perform the service efficiently while keeping the hair in optimum condition.

MEN'S COLOR DESIGN

LEARNING COLOR TECHNIQUES THAT APPEAL TO VARIOUS TYPES OF MALE CLIENTS WILL ALLOW YOU TO BROADEN YOUR COLOR CLIENTELE

FOLLOWING THIS LESSON

YOU WILL BE ABLE TO:

List various techniques that can be effectively performed to achieve varying effects for the male client

Describe the importance of communicating with the male client about color design

Demonstrate the knowledge and ability to perform color designs that are specifically designed with the male client in mind

Demonstrate the knowledge and ability to use techniques to reduce or cover gray hair

When designing color for your male clients, you will be faced with both opportunities and challenges. Although hair usually reacts the same way to color on male and female clients, that doesn't mean you can service them in the same way. Industry reports show that many male clients prefer to feel that certain salon services are specifically for men, and not just women's services performed on men. Many salons feature menus that contain services and descriptions designed with the male client in mind.

In *Chapter 4, Men's Color Design*, you will work with color techniques and designs that will appeal to different kinds of male color clients. Being able to offer these services as part of your color design repertoire will help you to expand your color clientele and build your revenue.

4.1 DESIGNING COLOR FOR MEN

The color techniques used on your male clients will often be very similar to those used on your female clients. In fact, in many cases the techniques might be exactly the same. However, what you need to consider when creating color designs for male clients is how you'll make subtle adaptations to better meet the male client's color demands. These demands very often include:

- Little to no upkeep or commitment
- Very natural, blended results
- No warm cast as the color fades over time
- A ruggedly handsome appearance that looks unintentional

MEN'S COLOR DESIGN TECHNIQUES

Male clients tend to fall into two categories—those who want their hair color to look as natural as possible and those who want their hair color to make more of a statement as part of their overall look. In the first category are the guys who want to look like their hair has been lightened by the sun and those who are prematurely gray or just want to look a little younger. In the second category are the guys who want to use their hair color as a way to express their personal style. Your approach to each of these clients will be key to gaining their confidence and loyalty.

The following pages show how you can adapt some of the techniques that you have learned to better suit your male clients, whether they prefer a "natural" look or want to make a bolder statement.

NATURAL EFFECTS

The men's color designs featured below are geared toward the male client who wants to achieve a natural look. Ideally, this client would want his hair to look like it has not been colored, or that any color variation occurred naturally.

The sun-kissed blond look or "surfer blond" is especially effective on medium to longer lengths. Multiple applications over time can create a more or less overall lightened effect.

The effect of a progression of highlights is achieved by reducing the size of the partings used in the interior. This places the individual highlights closer together. The interior appears lighter and brighter, which often happens naturally when the hair is exposed to the sun.

Not every client wants to completely cover his or her gray. Introducing darker-colored strands with customized placement can reduce the appearance of gray hair and add depth to a design.

Techniques such as painting, or using tools such as a Stryper Comb, will deposit color only on the selected strands and avoid a distinct line of demarcation as it grows out. Leaving the front hairline natural further softens the effect and increases wearability.

Other clients will want to completely cover their gray. This is especially true of a client who has grayed at an early age or who feels that he needs to look younger to be competitive in the job market.

An all-over, base-to-ends application is used to deposit color through the entire design. Because of shorter lengths and exposed hairlines, some male clients will require more frequent retouch appointments than female clients.

04

FASHION EFFECTS

Many male clients want to make a fashion statement and use their hair color design almost as an accessory—especially if they wear a strong hair sculpture. For these fashion-forward color designs, the structure of the hair sculpture plays an even greater role in the color design choices.

A single area of brighter color is used in this design to draw attention to the longer fringe lengths.

While the length alone may make the fringe a focal point of this sculpture, the addition of blond and reddish tones makes it a sure thing. Although the contrast in this design is quite strong, well-calculated color placement keeps it from overwhelming the sculpture.

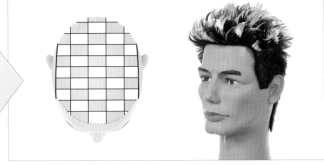

Endlights are used to draw attention to the interior lengths and sculpted texture of this design.

The highly texturized interior lengths of this short combination form are further enhanced by the addition of lighter tones to the ends in the interior. Concentrating these tones only at the hair ends in an alternating pattern increases the illusion of activation, since the darker base color subtly shows through.

GUIDELINES FOR MEN'S COLOR DESIGNING

As in any discipline, you may need to shift your communication style to be more aligned with the needs of the male hair color client. Although it is a growing market, it is still smaller than the female market. Paying special attention to how you communicate with this clientele will help you to build a solid reputation and a strong client base.

COMMUNICATION GUIDELINES

The following chart will help you respond to some of the more common male client cues in ways that encourage client trust, loyalty and open communication.

CLIENT CUE	DESIGNER RESPONSE
"I am thinking of highlighting my hair, but I hate when I see guys that look like they had their girlfriend use one of those at-home kits!"	*"I understand. You want your highlights to look less obvious and more natural, right? We'll discuss the options during the consultation to make sure that you are comfortable with the color of the highlights so that it is not too drastic for you. Then I'll place the highlights to make sure they mimic naturally highlighted hair as closely as possible."*
"I'm ready to get rid of some of my gray but not all of it! Can you do something that won't be so obvious when it grows out? I travel so much with my work that regular touch-ups may be too much of a hassle."	*"Sounds like a gray reduction or blending service would work best for you. I'll use a technique in which only the strands I select will be darkened to match your natural color. And none of the color will go all the way to the scalp, so you won't have an obvious line of new growth, especially if you have a little extra time between appointments."*
"I think I want to get rid of the gray completely—it's making me feel too old. But how can we make sure I don't end up looking like I got something at the drug store and dyed it myself?"	*"Two things that we need to look at: First, you have to understand the commitment you are making— at least while you choose to wear your hair darker. You'll have to keep regular retouch appointments. That will prevent the obvious regrowth and will also allow me to keep the color more uniform and balanced, avoiding the uneven color that results from the do-it-yourself method. Second, you can rest assured that I will formulate your color to look as natural as possible. If we do it right, no one will ever know that you have your hair colored."*
"I love this haircut, but my hair is so dark you can barely see how spiky it is. Can we do anything to make the texture more obvious?"	*"I have a great technique I can use that lightens only some of the ends and makes the texture really apparent. It is a really quick technique to use. I just sort of buff color onto the ends of your hair and that really punches up the texture that I have already sculpted."*

 # DEGREES OF GRAY

artist⁺access.

On the three heads below, which represent 100% gray, use markers
or colored pencils to indicate three different degrees of gray reduction.
Make sure each represents a natural-looking effect.

4.2 MEN'S COLOR DESIGNS

You are now ready to put into practice some of what you have learned about adapting your basic and advanced color skills for your male clientele. The male client can be quite particular about the results of a hair color service, so you'll want to be adept at using these techniques and others. As you gain experience in both technique and communication, your male clients will become some of the most loyal you'll have.

WORKSHOP 01
ALTERNATION – HIGHLIGHTS/ WEAVING

Highlights are an ideal way to add lighter tones while adding textural interest. A progression of highlight density is used to create a more natural effect, with more lighter tones in the interior.

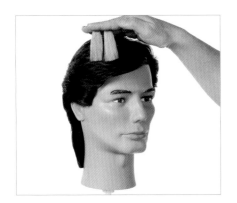

A progression of highlights is incorporated throughout this dark field using a medium-weaving technique. A violet-based toner is then applied over the entire head.

The finish shows an alternation of dark and light tones that enhances the texture. Fewer exterior highlights and more interior highlights create an overall progression in the design.

This color design is created on a planar form.

FORMULA: *Lightener with 20 volume (6%) developer.* TONER: *Level 8, violet-based demi-permanent color with 10 volume (3%) developer.*

The art shows the head sectioned vertically from the back of each ear over the crown. The front is sectioned with a wide center triangle extending from either recession area to the center crown. The back is sectioned with a vertical line through the center. Medium weaves will be used along horizontal partings in the back and front sections. Diagonal-back partings and medium weaves will be used in the side sections. One-inch (2.5 cm) partings will be used in the exterior and ½" (1.25 cm) partings will be used in the interior to create a progression.

01 Section the head into five sections as shown in the illustrations.

02-03 Begin on the right side of the nape. Release a 1" (2.5 cm) horizontal parting at the hairline. Then create a medium weave using the end of the tail comb. Position the foil at the scalp under the woven strands. Apply lightener to the hair from the edge of the foil to the ends.

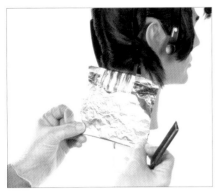 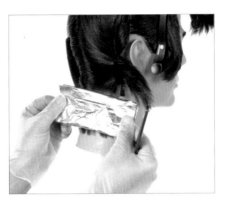 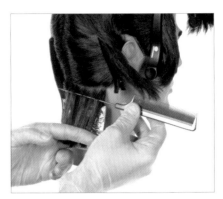

04-05 Use the double-fold technique, folding the foil approximately one-third upward, then folding up to the parting. Use the teeth of the comb to crease and fold each side inward.

06 Release the next 1" (2.5 cm) horizontal parting and repeat the weaving technique.

07 Apply lightener from base to ends and fold the foil. Continue to work upward.

08 When you reach the crest area, begin using ½" (1.25 cm) horizontal partings and continue using a medium-weave technique. As partings become wider, subsection and apply two foils to allow more control and proper color development. Weave, foil, and apply lightener onto one section and then the other.

09 Foil both sections evenly to avoid overlapping. Note that foils should be placed next to each other.

10-11 Work toward the top of the section. Note that you may need to subsection more than once in the widest area.

12 Continue the weaving and foiling techniques to complete the section.

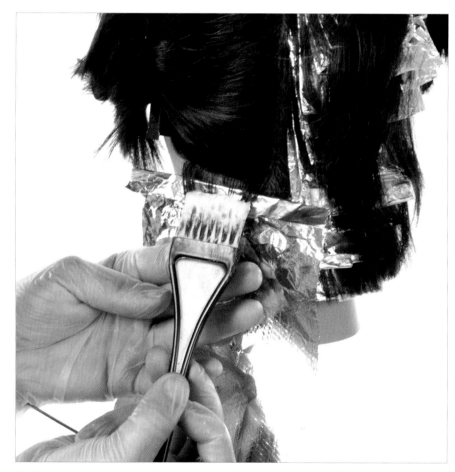

13 Next, move to the left side of the nape and use the same weaving and foiling techniques. Start at the hairline and use 1" (2.5 cm) horizontal partings in the area below the crest.

14-15 Work toward the top of this section. When you reach the crest area, use ½" (1.25 cm) horizontal partings and subdivide for control. Use two or more foils as needed.

16 Continue the weaving and foiling techniques to complete the back sections.

18 When you reach the recession area, begin to use ½" (1.25 cm) diagonal-back partings.

17 Next, move to one side and release a 1" (2.5 cm) diagonal-back parting at the bottom of the section. Weave the strands using a medium weave to be consistent with the back sections. Position the foil and apply lightener. Then fold the foil using the same technique used in the back.

19 Continue to apply lightener from the edge of the foil to the ends and use a double-fold technique.

20-21 Work toward the top of the section. Continue to subdivide to accommodate wider partings.

22 Complete this section. Then move to the opposite side and use the same techniques. Use 1" (2.5 cm) partings in the exterior and ½" (1.25 cm) partings in the interior.

23 Next, move to the front of the triangular section. Release a ½" (1.25 cm) horizontal parting at the front hairline, subdivide for control and use two or more foils as needed. Use the tail of the comb to create a medium weave. Note that ½" (1.25 cm) horizontal partings will be used throughout this section.

24 Apply lightener to one subsection and then the other.

25 Continue to work toward the back of the section.

26 Maintain even ½" (1.25 cm) partings and use consistent, medium weaves to complete the application.

27-28 Allow the lightener to develop until the desired degree of decolorization is achieved. Rinse thoroughly, then shampoo and dry the hair. Do not condition the hair at this point.

29 Apply toner to the entire head from base to ends. Process according to the manufacturer's instructions. Then rinse, shampoo, condition and finish as desired.

30-31 The finish shows the introduction of lighter colors, which creates the illusion of greater textural activation. The higher density of highlights in the interior creates a more natural effect.

ALTERNATION – HIGHLIGHTS/WEAVING

Draw or fill in the boxes with the appropriate answers.

artist**+**
access

EXISTING/DESIRED

E   E   E   E   E

D   D   D   D   D

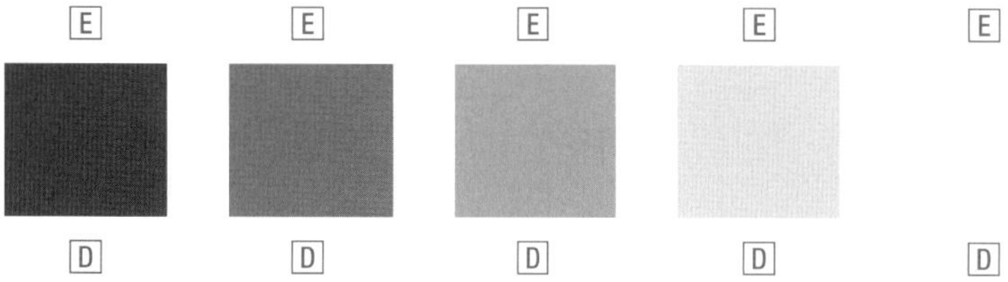

STRUCTURE

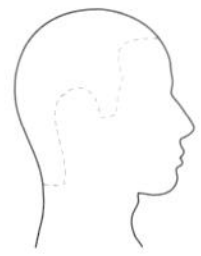

DESIGN PRINCIPLE

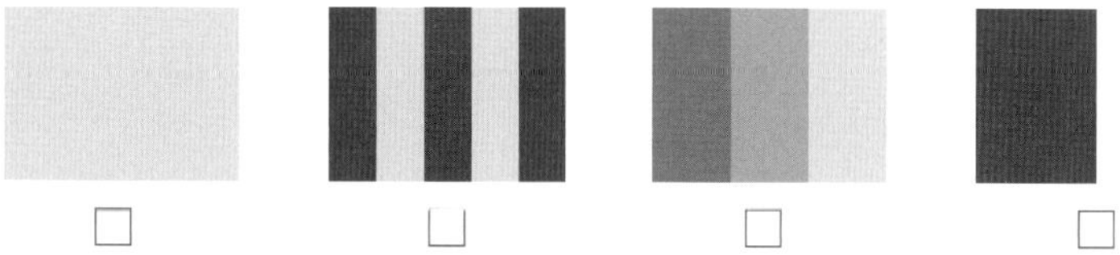

☐   ☐   ☐   ☐

FORM/TEXTURE

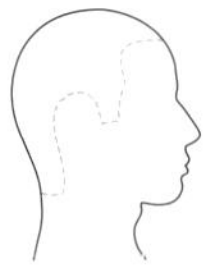

SECTIONING/PARTING PATTERN

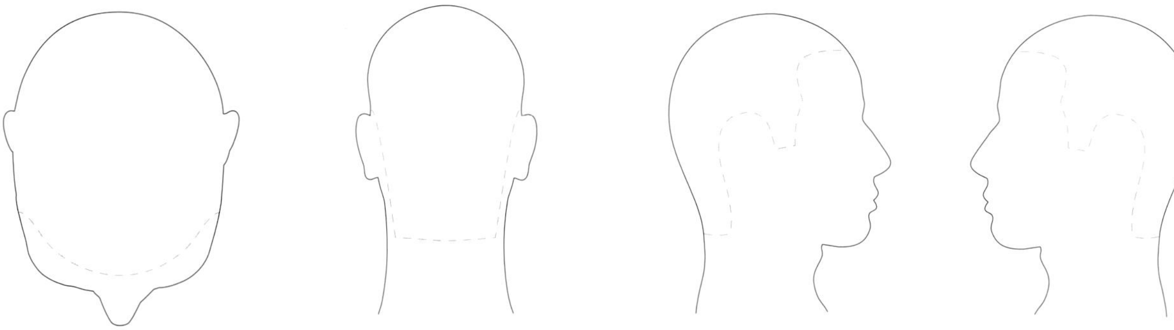

TOOLS/PRODUCT CHOICE

Educator Signature

Date

COLOR RUBRIC *WORKSHOP 01*
ALTERNATION – HIGHLIGHTS/WEAVING
This rubric is a performance assessment tool designed to measure your ability to
create *Pivot Point color designs.*

	LEVEL 1 *in progress*	LEVEL 2 *getting better*	LEVEL 3 *entry-level proficiency*
PREPARATION			
• Assemble color design essentials	☐	☐	☐
CREATE			
• Section head into five sections	☐	☐	☐
• Release 1" (2.5 cm) horizontal parting at hairline on right side of nape	☐	☐	☐
• Create a medium weave using end of tail comb	☐	☐	☐
• Position foil at scalp under woven strands	☐	☐	☐
• Apply lightener to hair from edge of foil to ends	☐	☐	☐
• Fold foil using a double-fold technique	☐	☐	☐
• Release next 1" (2.5 cm) horizontal parting and repeat same weaving technique	☐	☐	☐
• Apply lightener from base to ends and use same technique to fold foil	☐	☐	☐
• Continue to work upward using same technique	☐	☐	☐
• Begin using ½" (1.25 cm) horizontal partings in crest area; continue using medium weave	☐	☐	☐
• Subsection in wider areas; weave, foil, and apply lightener onto one section then the other	☐	☐	☐
• Foil both sections evenly; place next to each other	☐	☐	☐
• Continue to use same weaving and foiling techniques to complete section	☐	☐	☐
• Move to left side of nape; use 1" (2.5 cm) horizontal partings in area below crest; use same weaving and foiling techniques	☐	☐	☐
• Work toward top of section	☐	☐	☐
• Use ½" (1.25 cm) horizontal partings from crest; subdivide wider areas for control	☐	☐	☐
• Continue using same weaving and foiling techniques to complete back sections	☐	☐	☐
• Move to one side; release 1" (2.5 cm) diagonal-back parting at bottom of section	☐	☐	☐
• Weave strands using medium weave to be consistent with woven strands in back sections	☐	☐	☐

COLOR RUBRIC *WORKSHOP 01* (CONT'D)
ALTERNATION – HIGHLIGHTS/WEAVING

	LEVEL 1 *in progress*	LEVEL 2 *getting better*	LEVEL 3 *entry-level proficiency*
• Position foil; apply lightener; fold foil using same technique used in back	☐	☐	☐
• Use ½" (1.25 cm) diagonal-back partings at recession area	☐	☐	☐
• Continue to apply lightener from edge of foil to ends; use a double-fold technique	☐	☐	☐
• Use same techniques as you work toward top of section	☐	☐	☐
• Subdivide to accommodate wider partings	☐	☐	☐
• Complete section using same technique	☐	☐	☐
• Move to opposite side; use 1" (2.5 cm) partings in exterior and ½" (1.25 cm) partings in the interior	☐	☐	☐
• Move to front of triangular section; release a ½" (1.25 cm) horizontal parting at front hairline; subdivide wider areas for control; use tail of comb to create medium weave	☐	☐	☐
• Apply lightener using same weaving and foiling technique to one subsection, then the other	☐	☐	☐
• Continue to use same techniques working toward back of section	☐	☐	☐
• Maintain even ½" (1.25 cm) partings and use consistent, medium weaves to complete application	☐	☐	☐
• Process until desired degree of decolorization is achieved	☐	☐	☐
• Rinse, shampoo and dry hair	☐	☐	☐
• Apply toner to entire head from base to ends	☐	☐	☐
• Process according to manufacturer's instructions	☐	☐	☐
• Rinse, shampoo and condition hair	☐	☐	☐
• Finish as desired	☐	☐	☐

TOTAL POINTS = _____ + _____ + _____

TOTAL POINTS _____ ÷ HIGHEST POSSIBLE SCORE 111 X 100 = _____ %

Record your time in comparison with the suggested salon speed.

To improve my performance on this procedure, I need to:

_____   _____   _____
Student Signature   *Educator Signature*   *Date*

WORKSHOP 02
CONTRAST – ZONE/SLICING

Many clients would prefer to make a more progressive statement with their hair. In this color design, a strong contrast of colors complements the progressive sculpture.

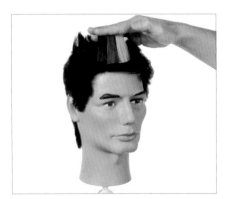

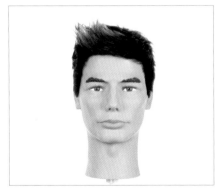

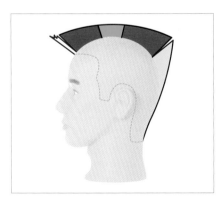

Light copper red and light blond colors are used within an interior zone to create a bold contrast in this color design. A darker color is applied to the remaining lengths of this dark field.

The finish shows striking color that enhances the longer interior lengths and directs the eye upward.

This color design is created on a combination form that features increase-layered and planar lengths at the top and gradated lengths at the sides and back.

FORMULA: *Lightener with 20 volume (6%) developer; level 8, copper red permanent color with 20 volume (6%) developer; level 2 brown permanent color with 10 volume (3%) developer.*

The art shows an off-center, triangle-shaped section parted just behind the front hairline. The corner over the left eye is rounded off. Medium-fine, back-to-back diagonal slices will be taken from the rounded corner of the triangular section. Note that the slices are wider toward the opposite side of the triangle.

01 Section a triangle-shaped section as shown in the illustration.

02-03 Begin at the front of the triangular section. Take a medium-fine diagonal slice starting at the rounded corner. Position a foil underneath the strand and apply a copper red color from the edge of the foil to the ends.

04 Fold the foil using the single-fold technique.

05-06 Release another diagonal slice from the rounded corner of the triangular shape and apply lightener using the same slicing and foiling techniques. Note that different colored foils are used to identify the lightener and the copper red color.

07 Continue the slicing and foiling techniques for the next three slices, applying lightener to each slice.

08 Release the last diagonal slice and apply the copper red color to complete this section.

09 Then gently clip the foiled sections up and out of the way.

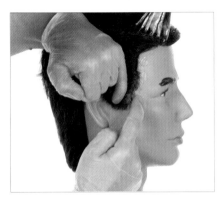

10 Next, apply barrier cream around the entire hairline and the tops of the ears.

11-12 Starting at the center nape, use a brush to apply the darker color vertically from base to ends. Work from the center to the right side, then from the center to the other side. Note that your finger may be used to control the lengths while applying color. You may need to alter your brush position to accommodate for the shorter perimeter lengths.

13 As you work upward, use the tail of the brush to part the longer lengths vertically. Work from the center toward one side. Direct shorter perimeter lengths back to avoid staining the skin.

14 Complete one side, then use the same techniques to complete the other side.

15 Move to the remaining top section and use horizontal partings to apply the darker color from base to ends. Work from the back toward the triangular section.

16 Take diagonal-back partings at the front perimeter hairline. Angle the brush to direct the hair back as you work toward the center. Repeat on the other side.

17 Process according to the manufacturer's instructions. Rinse the darker color first, then the copper red color and, finally, the lightener. Shampoo, condition and finish as desired.

18-20 The finish shows a bold contrast of color in which the longer, irregular layers become the focal point.

CONTRAST – ZONE/SLICING

Draw or fill in the boxes with the appropriate answers.

EXISTING/DESIRED

E   E   E   E   E

D   D   D   D   D

STRUCTURE

DESIGN PRINCIPLE

☐   ☐   ☐   ☐

FORM/TEXTURE

SECTIONING/PARTING PATTERN

TOOLS/PRODUCT CHOICE

Educator Signature

Date

COLOR RUBRIC *WORKSHOP 02*
CONTRAST – ZONE/SLICING
This rubric is a performance assessment tool designed to measure your ability to *create* *Pivot Point color designs.*

	LEVEL 1 *in progress*	LEVEL 2 *getting better*	LEVEL 3 *entry-level proficiency*
PREPARATION			
• Assemble sculpting essentials	☐	☐	☐
CREATE			
• Section off-center, triangle-shaped section with rounded corner behind front hairline	☐	☐	☐
• Begin at front of triangular section; take a medium-fine diagonal slice starting at rounded corner	☐	☐	☐
• Position foil underneath strand; apply copper red color from edge of foil to ends	☐	☐	☐
• Fold foil using single-fold technique	☐	☐	☐
• Release another diagonal slice from rounded corner of triangle shape	☐	☐	☐
• Apply lightener using same slicing and foiling techniques	☐	☐	☐
• Continue to use same slicing and foiling techniques for next three slices, applying lightener to each	☐	☐	☐
• Release last diagonal slice and apply copper red color using same application and foiling techniques to complete section	☐	☐	☐
• Gently clip foiled section up and out of the way	☐	☐	☐
• Apply barrier cream around entire hairline and tops of ears	☐	☐	☐
• Start at center nape; use brush to apply darker color vertically from base to ends	☐	☐	☐
• Work from center to right side, then from center to other side	☐	☐	☐
• Use tail of brush to part longer lengths vertically while working upward; continue to use same application technique	☐	☐	☐
• Work from center toward one side	☐	☐	☐
• Direct shorter perimeter lengths back to avoid staining the skin	☐	☐	☐
• Use same technique as you complete one side, then the other	☐	☐	☐
• Move to remaining top section; use horizontal partings to apply darker color from base to ends	☐	☐	☐
• Work from back toward triangular section	☐	☐	☐
• Take diagonal-back partings at front perimeter hairline	☐	☐	☐
• Angle brush to direct hair back while working toward center	☐	☐	☐
• Repeat same technique on other side	☐	☐	☐
• Process according to manufacturer's instructions	☐	☐	☐
• Rinse darker color first, then copper red and, finally, lightener; shampoo and condition	☐	☐	☐
• Finish as desired	☐	☐	☐

TOTAL POINTS = _____ + _____ + _____

TOTAL POINTS _____ ÷ HIGHEST POSSIBLE SCORE 75 X 100 = _____ %

Record your time in comparison with the suggested salon speed.

To improve my performance on this procedure, I need to:

Student Signature   Educator Signature   Date

WORKSHOP 03
PROGRESSION – GRAY REDUCTION

Gray reduction, sometimes referred to as gray blending, is ideal for clients who want to reduce their gray and maintain a look that grows out naturally. In this color design, lowlights are created using a Stryper Comb to apply a darker color to visually reduce the amount of gray.

Lowlights were introduced using a Stryper Comb technique to reduce the percentage of gray.

The finish shows a progression of gray reduction with more reduced in the back and less reduced in the front.

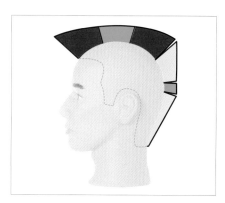

This color design is performed on a combination form that features a planar interior and a graduated exterior.

FORMULA: *Level 4, brown permanent color with 20 volume (6%) developer.*

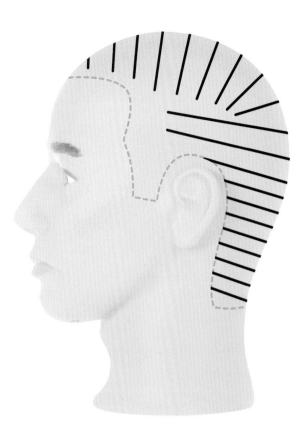

The art shows the approximate parting pattern that will be used in this design. The entire front hairline will be left natural. In the back and on the sides, ¼″ (.6 cm) slight diagonal-back partings will be used. In the interior, ½″ (1.25 cm) horizontal partings will be used. These partings will be adapted to the curve of the head in the crown. Partings will be taken as you work through the color design.

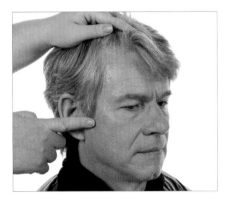

01 Apply barrier cream around the entire hairline and to the tops of the ears.

02 Beginning in the nape, take an approximate ¼″ (.6 cm) slight diagonal-back parting on the right side. Fill the reservoir of the Stryper Comb with the color.

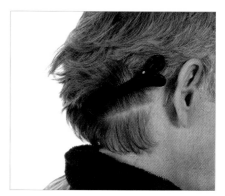

04 The results will be an alternation of color created within each subsection. Note that the Stryper Comb is applied to each subsection once but may be applied more than once for additional coverage.

03 Position the Stryper Comb parallel to the parting. Start with the tips of the teeth near the base and deposit color as you move to the ends.

05 Release another ¼″ (.6 cm) diagonal-back parting and repeat the same technique. Refill the Stryper Comb as needed.

06 Continue using consistent diagonal-back partings as you work to the back of the ear.

07 Use the same technique on the opposite side. Avoid disturbing the previously colored hair. Note that you can work from the center to the side or from the side toward the center.

08 Continue on one side, releasing a ¼″ (.6 cm) diagonal-back parting above the ear. Apply color, staying at least ½″ (1.25 cm) away from the front hairline.

09 Continue until partings extend to the recession area. Then repeat on the opposite side.

10 Move to the crown and use ½" (1.25 cm) partings that contour the curve of the head.

11 Use consistent partings as you work toward the front.

12 Partings will become horizontal as you work toward the front. You may choose to stand in front to make the application easier. At the front, do not extend partings to the sides. Apply color only to the center, leaving the front hairline natural to achieve a more natural finished look.

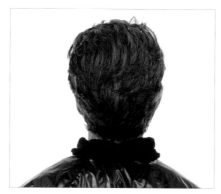

13-14 Process according to the manufacturer's instructions. Then rinse, shampoo, condition and finish as desired.

15 The finish shows a natural progression of gray coverage, which becomes more concentrated toward the back. This reflects a natural pattern of graying hair and also grows out more discreetly for the male client.

DESITN DECISIONS *WORKSHOP 03*

PROGRESSION – GRAY REDUCTION

Draw or fill in the boxes with the appropriate answers.

artist**+**
access.

EXISTING/DESIRED

E E E E E

D D D D D

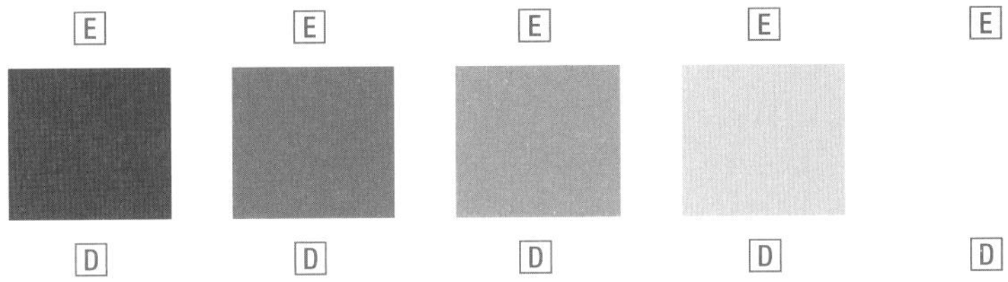

STRUCTURE

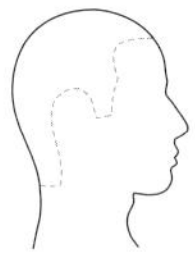

DESIGN PRINCIPLE

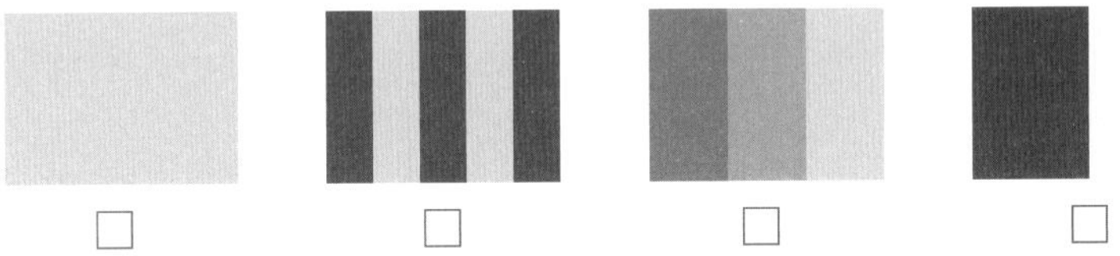

☐ ☐ ☐ ☐

FORM/TEXTURE

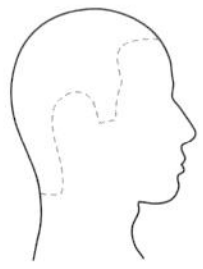

SECTIONING/PARTING PATTERN

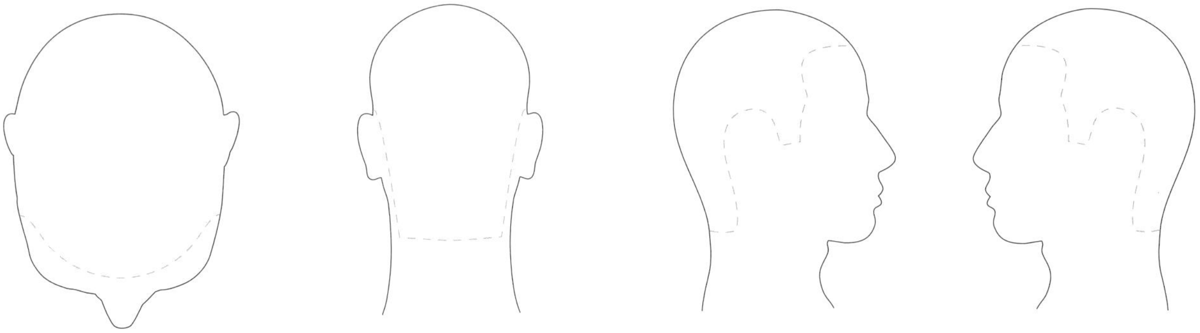

TOOLS/PRODUCT CHOICE

Educator Signature

Date

COLOR RUBRIC *WORKSHOP 03*
PROGRESSION – GRAY REDUCTION
This rubric is a performance assessment tool designed to measure your ability to create Pivot Point color designs.

	LEVEL 1 *in progress*	LEVEL 2 *getting better*	LEVEL 3 *entry-level proficiency*
PREPARATION			
• Assemble color design essentials	☐	☐	☐
CREATE			
• Apply barrier cream around entire hairline and tops of ears	☐	☐	☐
• Beginning in nape take an approximate ¼″ (.6 cm) slight diagonal-back parting on right side	☐	☐	☐
• Fill reservoir of Stryper Comb with color	☐	☐	☐
• Position Stryper Comb parallel to parting; move Stryper Comb through hair from base to ends	☐	☐	☐
• Release another ¼″ (.6 cm) diagonal-back parting; repeat same technique; refill Stryper Comb as needed	☐	☐	☐
• Continue using consistent diagonal-back partings working to back of ear	☐	☐	☐
• Use same technique on opposite side of nape; avoid disturbing previously colored hair	☐	☐	☐
• Continue on one side, releasing a ¼″ (.6 cm) diagonal-back parting above ear	☐	☐	☐
• Apply color using same technique, staying at least ½″ (1.25 cm) away from front hairline	☐	☐	☐
• Continue to use same technique until partings extend to recession area; repeat on opposite side	☐	☐	☐
• Move to crown; use ½″ (1.25 cm) partings that contour curve of head; use same technique to apply color	☐	☐	☐
• Use consistent partings and same technique working toward front as partings become horizontal	☐	☐	☐
• Apply color only to center at front; do not extend partings to sides	☐	☐	☐
• Leave front hairline natural	☐	☐	☐
• Process according to manufacturer's instructions	☐	☐	☐
• Rinse, shampoo and condition	☐	☐	☐
• Finish as desired	☐	☐	☐

TOTAL POINTS = _____ + _____ + _____

TOTAL POINTS _____ ÷ HIGHEST POSSIBLE SCORE 54 X 100 = _____ %

Record your time in comparison with the suggested salon speed.

To improve my performance on this procedure, I need to:

_____ _____ _____
Student Signature *Educator Signature* *Date*

REPETITION – GRAY COVERAGE

Some male clients choose to completely cover their gray hair to achieve a look that more closely resembles their natural color, prior to graying.

To cover this model's gray hair, a level 5, natural brown gold color is applied from base to ends.

The finished design shows a natural-looking color that has completely covered gray to replicate the model's natural color prior to graying.

This color design is performed on hair sculpted with the planar form in the interior and medium gradation in the exterior.

FORMULA: *Level 5, brown gold permanent color with 20 volume (6%) developer.*

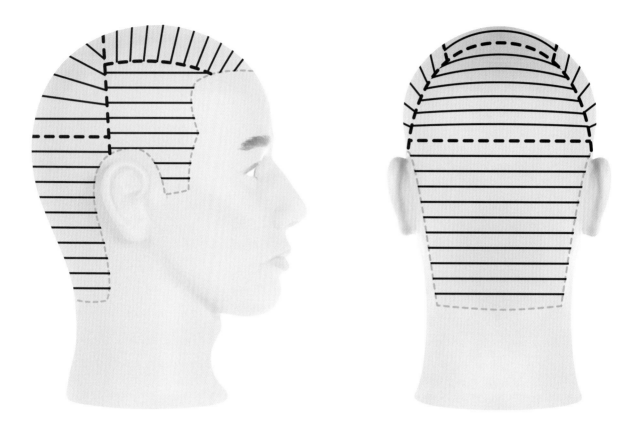

The art shows ¼″ (.6 cm) horizontal partings used throughout the back and top interior and horizontal partings on the sides. These short lengths do not require sectioning. These partings may be adapted to the curve of the head in the crown.

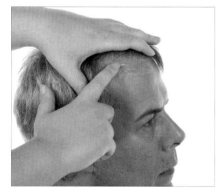

01 Apply barrier cream around the entire hairline.

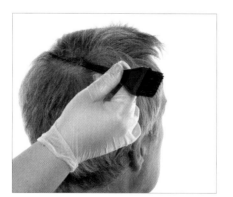 

02-03 Take a horizontal parting at the center crown area using the end of the color brush. Support the hair with a sculpting comb and apply color from base to ends.

04 Work from the center to one side and then to the other. Continue to support the hair with the sculpting comb and apply color from base to ends.

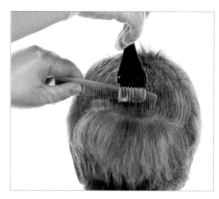

05 Work downward to the crest area. Continue adapting the partings to the curve of the head. Apply color from the center toward either side.

06 When you reach the crest, use the end of the color brush and lift the hair away from the scalp for better oxidation of the color.

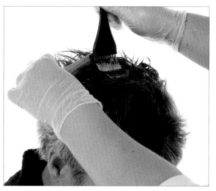

07 Next, move to the top and take a horizontal parting at the crown. Stand in front of the client, and work toward the front using the same technique to apply.

08 Continue taking horizontal partings working toward the front. Apply from the center toward the crest area on either side.

09 At the front hairline, apply carefully to avoid staining the scalp.

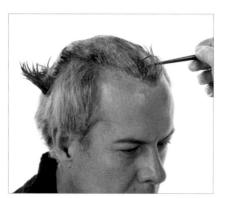

10 Use the end of the color brush to lift the lengths to allow color development.

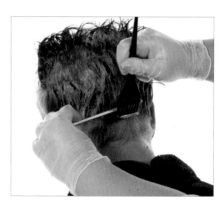

11 Move to the back exterior and use horizontal partings. Support the hair with the sculpting comb and apply color from base to ends, working from the center to either side.

12 Work toward the nape hairline. Apply carefully, then elevate the hair out and away from the scalp.

13 Move to the left side and use horizontal partings and the same application technique.

14 Apply color carefully, directing hair away from the face. At the sideburn, apply with upward strokes. Lift hair out and away from the scalp, then repeat on the opposite side.

15 Process according to manufacturer's instructions. Then rinse, shampoo, condition and finish as desired.

16 A natural-looking coverage of gray hair has given this client a refreshed look.

NOTE: *When the client's hair lengths are short, it is recommended to sculpt or trim hair after the color service if necessary.*

DESIGN DECISIONS *WORKSHOP 04*
REPETITION – GRAY COVERAGE
Draw or fill in the boxes with the appropriate answers.

artist**+**
access.

EXISTING/DESIRED

E E E E E

D D D D D

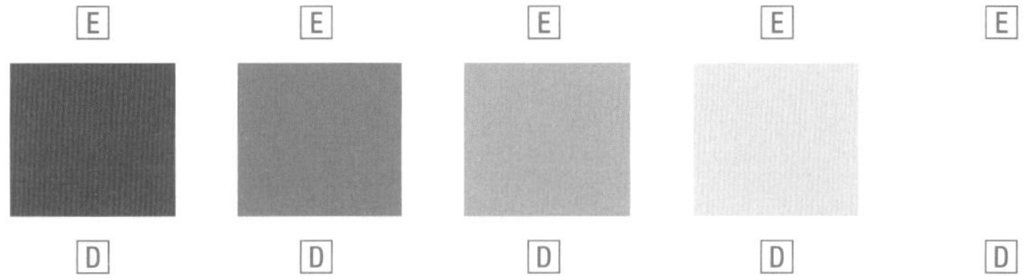

STRUCTURE

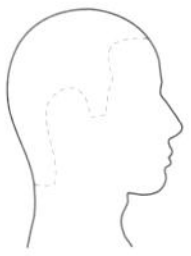

DESIGN PRINCIPLE

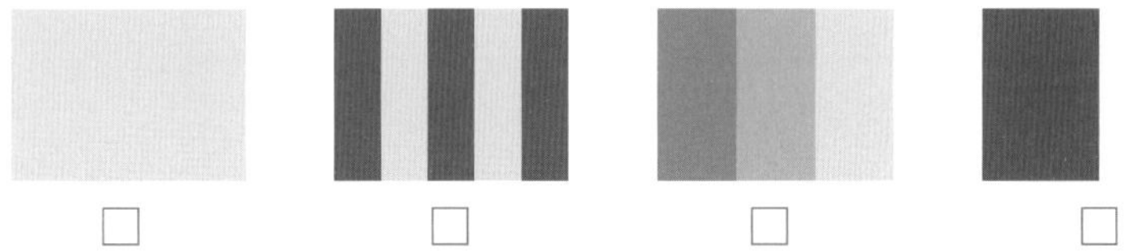

☐ ☐ ☐ ☐

FORM/TEXTURE

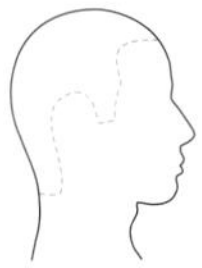

SECTIONING/PARTING PATTERN

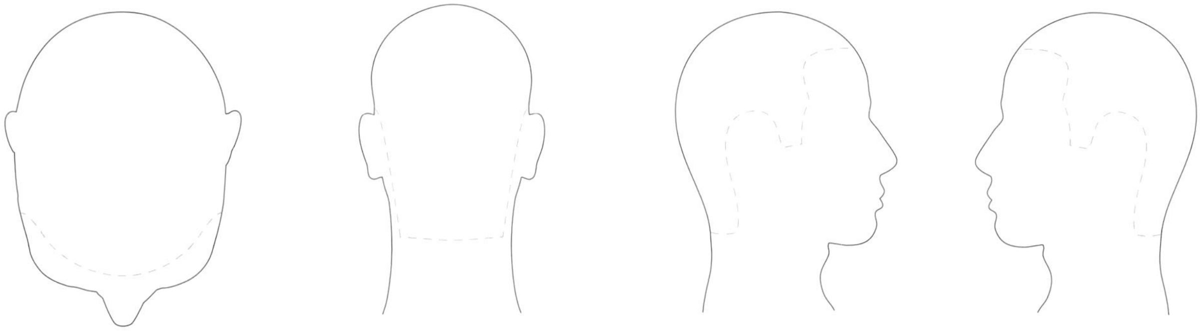

TOOLS/PRODUCT CHOICE

_____
Educator Signature   Date

COLOR RUBRIC *WORKSHOP 04*
REPETITION – GRAY COVERAGE

This rubric is a performance assessment tool designed to measure your ability to create Pivot Point color designs.

	LEVEL 1 in progress	LEVEL 2 getting better	LEVEL 3 entry-level proficiency
PREPARATION			
• Assemble color design essentials	☐	☐	☐
CREATE			
• Apply barrier cream around entire hairline	☐	☐	☐
• Take a horizontal parting in center crown; support hair with sculpting comb	☐	☐	☐
• Apply color from base to ends	☐	☐	☐
• Work from center to either side; continue to support hair with comb, applying color from base to ends	☐	☐	☐
• Work downward to crest area adapting partings to curve of head; apply from center to either side	☐	☐	☐
• Lift hair away from scalp using end of color brush	☐	☐	☐
• Move to top and take horizontal partings at crown; use same technique to apply	☐	☐	☐
• Continue working toward front using horizontal partings; work from center toward crest area on either side	☐	☐	☐
• Work toward front hairline; avoid staining scalp at front hairline	☐	☐	☐
• Lift hair away from scalp using end of color brush	☐	☐	☐
• Move to back exterior and apply using horizontal partings; work from center toward either side	☐	☐	☐
• Work toward nape hairline; elevate hair away from scalp	☐	☐	☐
• Move to left side and apply using horizontal partings and same application technique; direct hair away from face	☐	☐	☐
• Apply with upward strokes at sideburn	☐	☐	☐
• Lift hair up and away from scalp	☐	☐	☐
• Repeat on opposite side	☐	☐	☐
• Process according to manufacturer's instructions	☐	☐	☐
• Rinse, shampoo and condition	☐	☐	☐
• Finish as desired	☐	☐	☐

TOTAL POINTS = _____ + _____ + _____

TOTAL POINTS _____ ÷ HIGHEST POSSIBLE SCORE 60 X 100 = _____ %

Record your time in comparison with the suggested salon speed.

To improve my performance on this procedure, I need to:

_____   _____   _____
Student Signature   *Educator Signature*   *Date*

WORKSHOP 05
CONTRAST – ENDLIGHTS

Endlights can create the look of sun-kissed hair on clients with shorter lengths. Placing a lighter color at the ends of the hair can create a subtle or bold statement, depending on the contrast between the end and base colors.

This dark field is highlighted using lightener to achieve a light blond from the midstrand through the ends of the hair. A level 7, copper toner will then be applied to the entire head

This color design is created on a combination of high gradation and planar men's sculpture.

FORMULA: *Powder lightener with 20 volume (6%) developer.* TONER: *Level 7, copper, semi-permanent color.*

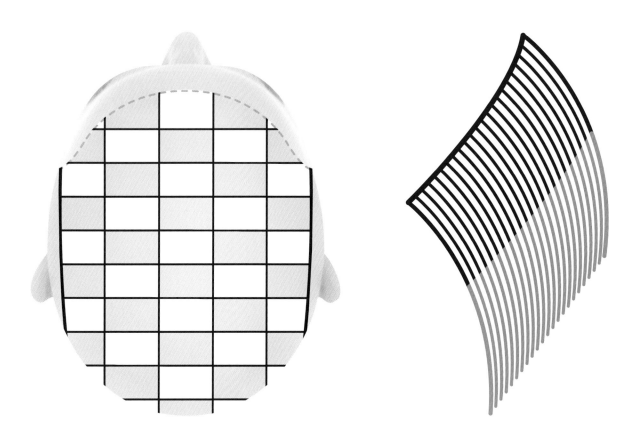

The art shows that color will be applied to the interior lengths from the back of the crown area to the front hairline. The staggered, or bricklay, pattern shown is used as a guide for this application. To produce endlights, color is applied only from the midstrand to the ends on selected strands. Note that the application can be more random, starting at slightly different points of the midstrand as you work to create a more blended, natural effect.

01 Prior to the color application, style the interior ends upward. This will allow greater control during application.

02-03 Begin in the back of the crown. Take a thin horizontal parting and clip the lengths above out of the way. Subdivide the parting and position your finger under the strands. On the right side of the parting, apply lightener away from the base to the ends. Apply lightener to another section of hair on the left side of the parting, leaving the middle of the parting untreated.

04 Release the next horizontal parting. Begin in the center of the parting. Work to either side to create a staggered or bricklay pattern.

05-06 Work toward the front. Avoid allowing the treated strands to come in contact with untreated hair. Complete the application of the lightener at the front hairline. Process until the desired degree of decolorization is achieved. Rinse, shampoo and towel-blot the hair thoroughly.

07 Apply the toner throughout the entire head. Process, rinse, shampoo and condition prior to styling.

08-09 The finish shows highlights positioned at the ends throughout the interior. The degree of lightening and the choice of toner will create more or less subtle effects.

CONTRAST – ENDLIGHTS
Draw or fill in the boxes with the appropriate answers.

artist**+**
access.

EXISTING/DESIRED

E   E   E   E   E

D   D   D   D   D

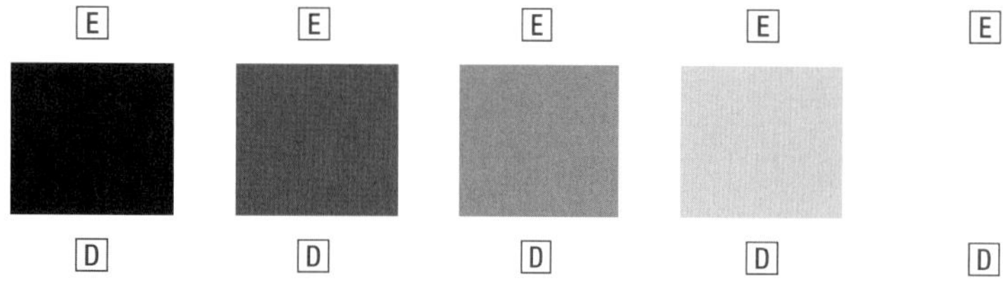

STRUCTURE

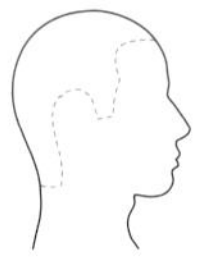

DESIGN PRINCIPLE

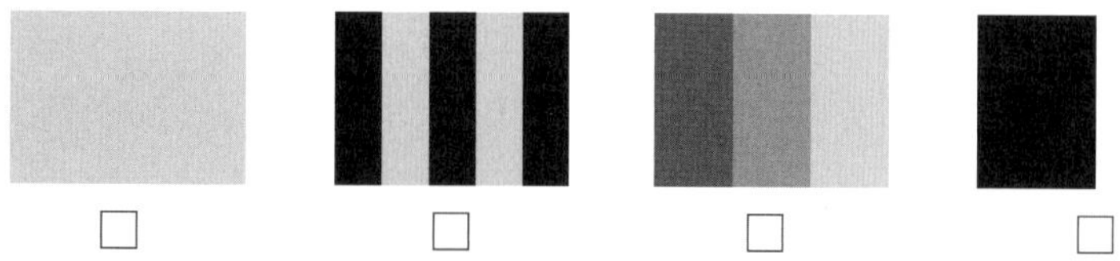

☐   ☐   ☐   ☐

FORM/TEXTURE

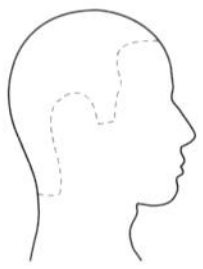

SECTIONING/PARTING PATTERN

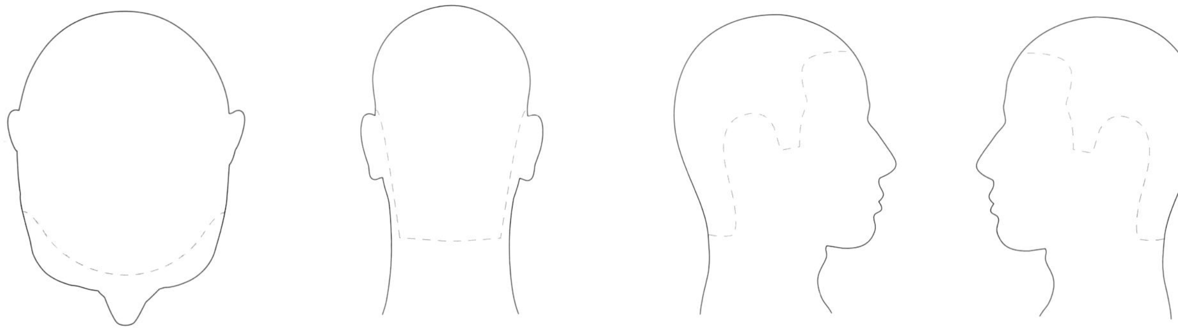

TOOLS/PRODUCT CHOICE

Educator Signature

Date

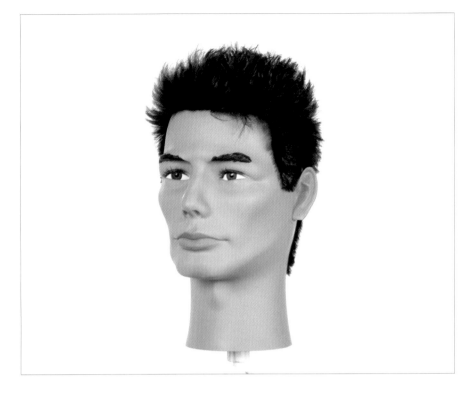

VARIATION 01
CONTRAST – ENDLIGHTS

This variation of the endlights technique uses lightener brushed onto a sheet of foil and then buffed across the surface of the hair. This technique can create a natural or an edgy look, and may be used with or without a toner.

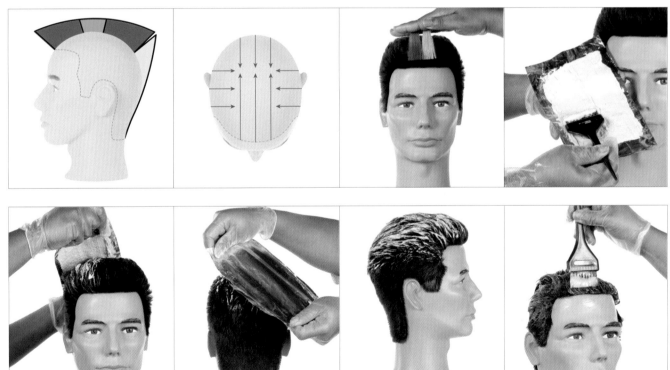

This endlight technique is performed on a dark field, high gradation and planar combination form. The hair is air formed to reflect the desired "spiky" finish. Then lightener is brushed evenly onto a piece of foil with a color brush. The foil is then lightly buffed across the surface of the interior beginning at the front hairline, working across the top of the head to the crown. More product is applied to the foil as needed. The same technique is used on the sides and back working from the crest toward the top of the head. The hair is processed to the desired degree of lightness, then rinsed, shampooed and towel-blotted thoroughly. Then toner is applied through the interior lengths and processed according to manufacturer's instructions. The hair is then rinsed, shampooed, conditioned and finished.

FORMULA: *Powder lightener with 20 volume (6%) developer.* TONER: *Level 7, violet semi-permanent color.*

COLOR RUBRIC *WORKSHOP 05*
CONTRAST – ENDLIGHTS
This rubric is a performance assessment tool designed to measure your ability to ***create*** *Pivot Point color designs.*

	LEVEL 1 *in progress*	LEVEL 2 *getting better*	LEVEL 3 *entry-level proficiency*
PREPARATION			
• Assemble color design essentials	☐	☐	☐
CREATE			
• Air form hair, styling interior ends upward	☐	☐	☐
• Take thin, horizontal partings starting at back crown; clip lengths above out of way	☐	☐	☐
• Subdivide parting; position finger under strands	☐	☐	☐
• Apply lightener away from the base to ends on right side of parting	☐	☐	☐
• Repeat application on another section of hair on left side of parting; leave middle of parting untreated	☐	☐	☐
• Release next horizontal parting; begin application at center to stagger	☐	☐	☐
• Work to either side applying product in a staggered or bricklay pattern	☐	☐	☐
• Work toward front using same techniques; work carefully to avoid having treated strands come in contact with untreated strands	☐	☐	☐
• Complete application of lightener at front hairline	☐	☐	☐
• Process to desired level of decolorization	☐	☐	☐
• Rinse, shampoo and towel-blot	☐	☐	☐
• Apply a level 7, copper toner throughout entire head	☐	☐	☐
• Process according to manufacturer's instructions	☐	☐	☐
• Rinse, shampoo and condition	☐	☐	☐
• Finish as desired	☐	☐	☐

TOTAL POINTS = _____ + _____ + _____

TOTAL POINTS _____ ÷ HIGHEST POSSIBLE SCORE 48 X 100 = _____ %

Record your time in comparison with the suggested salon speed. _____

To improve my performance on this procedure, I need to: _____

_____ _____ _____
Student Signature *Educator Signature* *Date*

VOICES OF SUCCESS

"I used to think that I wouldn't have a lot of male clients for hair color, but I was so wrong! I have learned how to work with my male clients—not just in terms of the application, but how I actually talk and consult with them. Now, the guys have become a large part of my color clientele."

THE DESIGNER

"It took me a long time—probably too long—to decide to color my hair and get rid of the gray. I am so glad that my colorist has the expertise to create something that looks natural and that keeps me looking as young as I want to. I depend on her for that."

THE CLIENT

"It makes sense to focus some of our marketing energy on the male hair color client. Quiet as that client may be, this is a market that we can't afford to ignore."

THE SALON OWNER

IN OTHER WORDS

Adapting hair color techniques and designs for the male client will help expand your client base and can create a loyal and steady clientele. As rewarding as some of the creative options can be, designing color for men who want to wear a natural design that calls no attention to itself can be just as satisfying.

LEARNING CHALLENGE

Circle the letter corresponding to the correct answer.

1. When designing color for the male client, it is important to remember that men tend to:
   a. like brighter colors
   b. spend more time on their hair
   c. have more time on their hands
   d. want color designs that are easy to maintain

2. To ensure that a color design for a male client looks natural:
   a. use reddish-brown tones
   b. use less contrast in the design
   c. use more contrast in the design
   d. color one level darker than the natural color

3. Generally, the two effects that a male client may want to achieve are a natural effect and:
   a. a fashion effect
   b. looking younger
   c. looking more distinguished
   d. making a bold color statement

4. To create the look of sun-kissed, natural highlights, apply:
   a. less to the interior
   b. more highlights at the sides
   c. more highlights in the interior
   d. highlights evenly throughout the head

5. Gray reduction or gray blending positions darker tones:
   a. only in the interior
   b. only along the front hairline
   c. from base to ends throughout
   d. along selected strands to achieve a natural effect

LESSONS LEARNED

- Male clients generally fall into two groups: those who want their hair color to look natural and those who want to make a fashion statement.

- When coloring a male client's hair, designers often give special consideration to achieving results that need little to no upkeep, are very natural and blended, don't fade into warm casts and create a ruggedly handsome appearance that looks unintentional.

- Communicating effectively with the male client will help you to make the most appropriate design decisions for each client.

- Men's color designs require a step-by-step process that incorporates the use of basic and advanced techniques and patterns and adapts them to fit the male client's needs.

ADAPT AS A DESIGNER

With all your newly gained color design skills, your next challenge is to expand your ability to select and create color designs that are appropriate and flattering to best suit your clients. Once you truly understand how hair color relates to the sculpture and the overall hair design, you'll quickly realize that a hair design without color is very much like a black-and-white photograph. Understanding the transformation possibilities in addition to the skills and techniques to use will allow you to achieve amazingly beautiful outcomes.

Adapting color design has two components: composing and personalizing. Composing involves integrating all your knowledge, skills and vision to create a single new color design. When you compose a color design, you show that you understand how your design decisions and techniques yield the results you envision. Personalizing the design helps ensure that it is appropriate and flattering to each client.

By changing the pattern, creating a focal point and altering the surface texture, you can accentuate specific features or de-emphasize others. As you continue learning to adapt color, you will become comfortable using different sources of inspiration and making design decisions that produce predictable results. Within the pages of Pivot Point's *Meta* collections, examples of dynamic color designs created by adapting as a designer may also serve as inspiration. As you look through *Meta*, you will recognize that almost anything you visualize can be realized through adapting. Elevating your work from "satisfactory" to "breathtaking" is why adapting as a designer reflects the ultimate in professional color design.

Now you can start developing your ability to adapt color as a designer. A personal portfolio where you will store "before-and-after" photographs can be a great tool for tracking your success. Keep notes describing your thought process for adapting color designs. Note the techniques used, what worked well, what didn't work well, and what you might have done differently. Your portfolio provides the chance for you to monitor your growth as a designer and your proficiency at adapting. Your portfolio provides the chance for you to monitor your growth as a designer and your proficiency at adapting.

TERMS

Apply – Method of distributing a color product onto strands.

Base – Portion of hair shaft, from the scalp up to 1" (2.5 cm) upward; the area of the strand where color is most often applied during a retouch.

Base-to-Ends Application – The technique of applying a color product from the base throughout the ends; generally used during a virgin-darker application to add tone or darken existing hair color.

Color – The visual perception of the reflection of light.

Colorist – Cosmetologists who specialize in creating color designs.

Color Along the Strand – The technique of applying a color product to specific area(s) of the hair strand.

Color Levels – Categories of color that identify the lightness or darkness of a color.

Color Placement – The position or placement of one or more colors within a color design as it relates to an area of the head or along the strand.

Combination Form Color Designing – The process of designing color by adapting color placement to best suit the structure of the sculpted combination form present.

Complementary Colors – Colors found opposite one another on the color wheel; in hair color, they neutralize or cancel out one another when mixed together; used to neutralize unwanted tones.

Cool – A term used to describe a color with an absence of warmth. Also described as ash or drab; violet, blue and green ranges of the color wheel.

Decolorize – The process of lightening the hair's natural pigment.

Deposit – The addition of color pigment to darken or add tone to the hair.

Desired Color – The field and shade of color agreed upon by the client and colorist prior to the color design service.

DESIGN PRINCIPLES

Artistic arrangement patterns for the design elements of form, texture and color to follow.

Alternation – Design principle that is a sequential repetition where two or more units occur in a repeating pattern; can break up the surface of an object and create interest.

Contrast – Design principle in which desirable relationships of opposites occur; creates a variety and stimulates interest in a design; colors that are either warm or cool or at least three levels apart.

Progression – Design principle in which all units are similar, but gradually change in an ascending or descending scale; leads the eye rhythmically within a design; a gradual change in color in an ascending or descending scale.

Repetition – Design principle in which all units are identical except for positions; creates a feeling of uniformity; one color repeated within a given area or throughout.

Develop – The time frame required for color products to achieve the intended result; also referred to as processing time.

Double-Process Technique – Two-step hair color process that involves lightening (decolorizing) the hair first and then adding color (recolorizing) the hair to achieve the desired results.

Existing Color – The color(s) present in the hair prior to the color design service; acts as underlying pigment.

Fields of Color – Categories of color; light, medium and dark further divided into medium light and medium dark.

Focal Point – Selective placement of contrasting color that attracts the eye to a specific area in a design.

Foiling – A method of highlighting or lowlighting, using foil to isolate the strands of hair to be lightened, colored, or protected with conditioner.

Highlighting – A technique by which selected woven or sliced strands of hair are lightened.

Intensity – The vividness, brightness or saturation of a color within its own level; strength of tone.

Level – Also known as value or depth; the degree of lightness or darkness of a hair color relative to itself and other colors; identified on a scale of 1 to 10 or 1 to 12, with 1 being the darkest (black) and 10 (or 12) the lightest (lightest blond).

Line of Demarcation – Location where an obvious difference between two colors occurs along a hair strand; a visible line of separation; a line separating colored hair from new growth.

Lowlighting – A technique by which selected woven or sliced strands of hair are darkened.

Overlapping – Occurs when the application of a color or lightener extends over previously treated hair; can result in bands of color or breakage depending on the product used.

Part – To create lines that subdivide shapes or sections of hair for better control and accuracy while applying color.

Partial Highlights – Technique that results in highlights in a specific area of the head, usually in the interior.

Pigment – Color, either natural or artificial.

Porosity – The ability of the hair to absorb and hold moisture, liquids and chemicals; can be classified as average, resistant, extreme, or uneven.

Predisposition Test – A skin test to determine an individual's over-sensitivity to certain chemicals; also known as a patch, allergy or skin test. Used 24 to 48 hours prior to a permanent hair color service.

Process – The time it takes a color product to work and/or develop.

Remove and Condition – Thoroughly rinsing color product from the hair and scalp, often followed by shampooing and a conditioning treatment, which achieves optimum, long-lasting color results.

Retouch Application – The application of color or lightener to the new growth of hair only to match the existing color.

Scrunching – Technique used to apply color with a finger-application method; involves gently squeezing the color product onto the hair ends.

Section – Color design step that divides the hair into workable areas for control and color placement; often relating to the structure of the sculpture.

Shapes – Individual sections of hair used to further break down sections or zones; described by geometric shapes.

Slicing – Technique used to isolate straight partings to be treated with color or lightener.

Strand Test – Performed during the processing of a color application to monitor processing time and to assess any stress to the hair or scalp.

Tonality – Term used to describe whether the color is cool, neutral or warm.

Tone – The warmth or coolness of a color; also known as hue or the name of the color.

Virgin Hair – Hair that has not received previous chemical services.

Warm – A term used to describe a color containing red, orange or yellow.

Weaving – Technique used to isolate strands to be treated with color or lightener; employs a zigzag movement of the tail of the comb to selected strands; the resulting woven strand can be classified as fine, medium or thick.

Zonal Pattern – Segmented areas (zones) of a design that are colored separately; generally used in the fringe, crown and/or nape.

Zones – Segmented areas of a design that are colored separately.

COLOR PRODUCT TERMS
Products used to color the hair.

Ammonia – Used in hair color to swell the cuticle; when mixed with hydrogen peroxide, activates the oxidation process of melanin and allows melanin to decolorize; strong alkaline solution that enables an oxidative color product to decolorize hair pigment and develop new color.

Barrier Cream – Used to avoid staining and to protect the client's skin; also used to protect hair to remain untreated.

Catalyst – An oxidizing agent, generally very low-volume hydrogen peroxide.

Developer – An oxidizing agent, most frequently hydrogen peroxide, at an acidic pH that is mixed with oxidative hair colors and lighteners to decolorize hair, increase porosity and develop color molecules; the concentration of hydrogen peroxide in a water solution; expressed as volumes of oxygen liberated per volume of solution; also expressed in percentages.

5 vol = 1.5%
10 vol = 3%
20 vol = 6%
30 vol = 9%
40 vol = 12%

Intensifier – Undiluted color that can be added to any oxidative or nonoxidative color to enrich, intensify or tone down a color.

NONOXIDATIVE HAIR COLORS

Hair coloring products that deposit pigment without oxidation and do not decolorize the hair's natural pigment.

Semi-Permanent Hair Color – A nonoxidative hair color that slightly penetrates the hair shaft and lasts through several shampoos.

Temporary Hair Color – Nonoxidative hair color that coats the outside of the hair and usually washes out after one or two shampoos.

OXIDATIVE HAIR COLORS

Hair coloring products that can lighten and/or deposit color and require the addition of a developer (usually hydrogen peroxide) for the color to process.

High-Lift Tint – Color with the ability to lift natural melanin 3-5 levels and deposit delicate tones; single-process color with a higher degree of lightening action and minimum amount of color deposit.

Lightener – A product used to decolorize natural pigment; also known as bleach; powder lightener is generally an off-the-scalp product; cream, oil or gel lighteners are designed for use on or off-the-scalp.

Long Lasting Semi-Permanent Hair Color – Often referred to as demi-permanent color; generally does not contain ammonia; deposit-only colors.

Permanent Hair Color – Also known as oxidative hair color or tint; a product that requires an oxidizing agent to create a chemical reaction in order to change hair color; the resulting color lasts until it grows out or is cut off.

Toner – A pastel color designed for use on hair that has been decolorized to the lightest levels.